Day by Day with Saint Benedict

Day by Day
with Saint Benedict

Terrence G. Kardong, O.S.B.

LITURGICAL PRESS
Collegeville, Minnesota

www.litpress.org

Cover design by Joachim Rhoades, o.s.b. *Saint Benedict,* fresco, 14th century, Basilica di S. Maria, Pomposa, Italy. Photo courtesy of Cameraphoto Arte, Venice/Art Resource, New York.

1	2	3	4	5	6	7	8

Library of Congress Cataloging-in-Publication Data

Kardong, Terrence.
    Day by day with Saint Benedict / Terrence G. Kardong.
        p.   cm.
    Summary: "Daily reflections for religious and lay persons on the
    Rule of St. Benedict and the Benedictine life"—Provided by publisher.
    Includes bibliographical references and index.
    ISBN 13: 978-0-8146-3042-6 (pbk. : alk. paper)
    ISBN 10: 0-8146-3042-1 (pbk. : alk. paper)
        1. Benedict, Saint, Abbot of Monte Cassino. Regula—Meditations.
    2. Devotional calendars.   I. Title.

BX3004.Z5.K345 2005
255'.106—dc22

                                                              2004027584

Contents

Preface

When I was asked by the Liturgical Press to write daily meditations on the Rule of St. Benedict, I was not too enthusiastic. My first thought was a coffee-table book, and that seemed beneath my dignity as a scholar. But then I reflected that such a book need not be superficial. It would be entirely up to me whether it would be shallow or substantial. Another thought that nagged at the back of my mind was the brute fact that there are 365 or 366 days in the year. Do I have that much to say?

Well, of course, I do have a lot to say or at least I can say a lot. That was shown by the large (641 pp.) commentary I had recently put out on the same Rule of St. Benedict.[1] Since this was also published by the Liturgical Press, no doubt they wanted me to transform my scholarly thoughts into something a bit more manageable for the ordinary person. Such a prospect is not always attractive to the scholar, but it does have the useful function of making him come down to earth. I don't think my commentary is particularly inaccessible, but I recognize that it needs to be applied to daily life. I have tried to do that in these meditations.

Now there are many ways of accomplishing the hermeneutical task of translating exegesis into practical commentary. One of the best ways is through story, and I have told a few in these pages. They are all "true" stories that come from my long experience of Benedictine community life. The names are changed, but they really happened. I know a lot more stories, but most

---

[1] Terrence G. Kardong, o.s.b., *Benedict's Rule: A Translation and Commentary* (Collegeville: Liturgical Press, 1996).

of them would take too long to tell in the format allotted to this book. Nevertheless, I recognize that many readers would probably prefer more concrete narrative and less generalization.

But the bulk of the book is given over to more abstract attempts to apply the ancient monastic wisdom to the conditions of modern monasteries. That implies that I know two things: (1) What the original text really means; (2) What modern monastic life is like. As to the first question, I tried to answer it in a systematic way in my commentary entitled *Benedict's Rule.* But regarding the second, I can only say that I have been a Benedictine since 1956 and I have lived in monasteries throughout the world. So I have a fair idea of "life on the ground." I also have my own ideas of what modern monastic life *should* be like. If I did not, it would be a waste of time writing books like this one.

Since these commentaries are all based on the text of Benedict, it is no surprise that they are also based on my previous exegetical studies. I am primarily a literary scholar, and so I always tend to approach texts in that manner. In this particular writing project, my habitual method was to consult my own commentary to "find out what I know." Then only would I venture to say "what it means." That being the case, I really can make little claim for originality in these pages. Anybody who cares to plow through my big book will find all my ideas there; yet here they are distilled into a more concentrated, and perhaps more palatable, form.

Was writing this book a good experience? Better than I hoped. Of course, the format itself guaranteed a certain amount of tedium. I found out existentially what I had previously only known vaguely, namely, that there are very many days in a year. In practical terms, that meant I simply had to mine that many *ferverinos* out of the ancient Rule. Since meditations are supposed to be inspiring, this seems to imply that the writer will feel deeply enough about the subject to inspire the audience. In an ideal world, that might suggest that the author would brood long over a given passage, eventually erupting in a volcano of fervor. As a matter of fact, I often sat at the computer grinding out unit after unit. As someone once said, inspiration is often a matter of perspiration.

Yet I would still claim that some of these little meditations *are* deeply felt. I am not just a student of Benedict; I am his disciple! His Rule is what I live by, not just what I dissect. But besides my religious profession, I like to think my "objective," "neutral" research feeds my passion. To study a classic text year after year, indeed for a lifetime, is to become so familiar with it that at least parts of it become indistinguishable from one's own mind and heart. And so when I come to those passages, such as RB 72, I think I "wax eloquent." But there are other tracts of the text where all I can do is to trudge along, hoping to find a scrap of inspiration here and there. A glance at the index will show that I don't have much to say about the liturgical chapters (RB 9–18) and the ones on penalties (RB 23–30).

What about the random arrangement of the texts? I do not simply march through the Rule, beginning with Prologue 1 on January 1. Why not? Perhaps because I thought it would give the book the appearance of another commentary, which it is not. Well, then why not key the passages to the particular dates of the calendar? What text of RB would you suggest for Christmas? For the Fourth of July? Finally, I decided to simply scatter the units all over the calendar. Of course, one disadvantage with this is that one loses whatever context there would be with a consecutive approach. But at least there is the element of surprise—you never know what you will run into on the next page. And I hope the units are sufficiently self-contained to be intelligible to the general reader.

And so the job is done. In fact, I am grateful I was able to complete it. Since I began it last year I have contracted a serious illness which made me wonder if I would ever finish. Thanks be to God, the doctors have provided me with medication that makes life interesting and work possible (which are pretty much the same thing for me). Any regrets? Oh yes, I would have liked to polish each little unit into a perfect gem. But life is not long enough for that. I am no Pascal. Besides, sometimes the "best is the enemy of the good." If I can make life a bit more hopeful for a few people through these words, they are not wasted.

To close with a word about issues of translation and gender. Wherever possible I have used recognized modern translations of the Bible. But when I am translating Benedict's Latin I do not, because he is *not* using any standard translation. To conform his translation to modern criteria often distorts his argument. I have followed the translation I did in *St. Benedict's Holy Rule for Public Reading. Male and Female Versions* (Richardton, N.D.: Assumption Abbey, 2003). In regard to gender, I have tried to be even handed. But since the Rule is written in the masculine form this is not always easy or even possible. It is hard to satisfy everybody: someone pointed out that my use of the masculine pronoun for Satan is not exactly fair.

T.G.K.

References and Abbreviations

Basil of Caesarea. Long Rules. In *Ascetical Works,* vol. 1.; Fathers of the Church, 9 New York: Fathers of the Church; [Washington, D.C.: Catholic University Press, 1950]. Latin Rule in Migne, J.-P. *Patrologiae cursus completus (PL),* vol. 103.483ff.

Cassian, John. *Conferences (Conf.).* Trans. Boniface Ramsey in Ancient Christian Writers, 57. New York: Paulist Press, 1997. *Institutes (Inst.)* Trans. Boniface. Ramsey, Ancient Christian Writers, 58. New York: Newman, 2000.

Cyprian. *On the Lord's Prayer (LP).* In *The Letter of St. Cyprian of Carthage.* Trans. G. W. Clark. Ancient Christian Writers, 20. New York; Ramsey N.J.: Paulist Press, 1984.

De Vogüé, Adalbert. *La Règle de Saint Benoît.* 6 vols. Paris: Cerf, 1972.

History of the Monks in Egypt. The ancient travelogue entitled *Historia Monachorum in Aegypto* is translated under the title *The Lives of the Desert Fathers* by Norman Russell. Kalamazoo, Mich.: Cistercian Publications, 1981.

Kardong, Terrence G. *Benedict's Rule: A Translation and Commentary* (BR) Collegeville: Liturgical Press, 1996.

Lentini, Anselmo. *La Regola / S. Benedetto; testo, versione e commento* 2nd ed. Montecassino: [The Abbey] 1980. 1st ed., 1950.

Lives of the Fathers. Trans. Owen Chadwick. In *Western Asceticism.* Philadelphia: Westminister, 1958.

Pachomius. *The Life of Pachomius* in *The Life of Saint Pachomius and his Disciples.* Trans. Armand Veilleux., Pachomian Koinonia, vol. 1. Cistercian Studies Series, vol. 45. Kalamazoo, Mich.: Cistercian Publications, 1980. G1 refers to the First Greek Life; Sbo refers to the Coptic Life. The Rule of Pachomius is in *Pachomian Chronicles and Rules. Koinonia.* Trans. Armand

Veilleux. Pachomian Koinonia, vol. 2. Cistercian Studies Series, vol. 46. Kalamazoo, Mich.: Cistercian Publications, 1982.

BR   See Kardong, above.

Prol.   Prologue (in Benedict or Pachomius).

RA   The Rule of St. Augustine. In Augustine, *Letters*. Trans. Sr. Wilfrid Parsons. Writings of Saint Augustine, vol. 13; Fathers of the Church, 32. New York: Fathers of the Church; [Washington, D.C.: Catholic University Press] 1956. Other translations are also readily available.

RB   Rule of Benedict

RM   *The Rule of the Master.* Trans. Luke Eberle. Cistercian Studies Series, vol. 6. Kalamazoo, Mich.: Cistercian Publications, 1977.

Thema Pater. Commentary on the Our Father and part of the Prologue of the Rule of the Master.

January 1

We said that all are to be summoned to counsel because the Lord often reveals what is best to the younger. (RB 3.3)

The sixth century was not a time of youth culture. Young people were meant to be seen and not heard. Consequently, it was quite natural that they be ignored at community meetings. Before my first chapter meeting, an old monk said to me, half-jokingly: "We usually don't speak in here for the first ten years." But Benedict will not hear of this. For him, it violates the biblical principle that the Holy Spirit can speak to whomever she pleases. In Matthew 11:25 we read: "I give praise to you, Father, Lord of heaven and earth, for although you have hidden these things from the wise and the learned you have revealed them to the childlike" (NAB). This, of course, does not mean that the young should thrust themselves forward in any brassy way. Monasteries where only the elders have the floor tend to become bastions of conservatism and stagnation. As one monk said about his ancient European monastery: "The trouble with this place is that the archives are a thousand years old and everybody knows what is in them."

January 2

Since we read that our holy fathers performed the whole psalter with great labor in one day, let us, despite our lukewarmness, at least do so in a whole week! (RB 18.25)

In this verse, Benedict is trying to shame his disciples into reciting the whole psalter every week. And he does it by means of a kind of "golden age" argument: since the ancients did such and such, we should at least do such and such. Now there is nothing wrong with such thinking, but one should recognize it for what it is—and it is not history! In other words, the earliest monks certainly did *not* recite the whole psalter in a day. If they had, it would have taken all day and they would have starved to death. The writings of Cassian (*Inst.* 2.5) include a vision by an angel in which Pachomius is instructed not to recite more than twelve psalms at the night Office. In a similar passage, Benedict claims that the old monks never drank wine (RB 40.6) but the Desert literature of Egypt indicates that they did. We should take this rhetoric for what it is worth, not for cold cash.

January 3

Let (the cellarer) take good care of all the abbot entrusts to him, but not meddle in what is withheld from him. (RB 31.15)

Here we see one of Benedict's typical themes come into play: an official is warned not to usurp more power than is rightly his. In Benedict's usual language, this is "presumption," the arrogation of power that is not one's own. In the case of the cellarer, the limits are clearly spelled out. He is to care for all that is entrusted to him but not intrude into what is not so entrusted. So it is a question of boundaries and their observance. Certainly, Benedict does not want his cellarer gradually extending his "territory" until he has his finger in everything. When that happens, "fingers need to be slapped." It would seem that this office demands a special kind of humility, to play such a role properly. The cellarer must carry a good deal of responsibility, but he can never claim absolute control over the system in which he works. Many people in the world cannot work with those restrictions; they should not become cenobites —members of a monastic community.

January 4

Monks ought to strive for silence at all times, but especially during the night hours . . . when they leave Compline, no one has permission to say anything more to anybody . . . Exceptions to this rule occur when the guests need something or the abbot commands someone to do something. (RB 42.1, 8, 10)

We live in a deafening society, and even though nature itself quiets down for the night, we do not. We turn up the volume. Benedict wants to hear a pin drop in the hours between Compline and Matins (roughly 7 p.m. to 6 a.m.). Certainly he sees this as prime time for recollection and he wants to create the conditions that promote it. Yet there are exceptions. For example, charity comes before silence. Our guests have needs that must be met, and we should not fail to meet these needs on the grounds of silence. Further, obedience may have to be elevated over silence when the case demands. In one of his books, Thomas Merton tells of the time that a dead brother was allowed to lie untended all night in the dormitory, presumably to protect the night silence. It is doubtful Benedict would sanction that kind of behavior.

January 5

When [the prioress] corrects someone, she should act prudently and not overreact. If she scours the rust too hard, she may break the vessel. Let her always be wary of her own fragility and remember not "to break the bent reed" [Isa 42:3]. (RB 64.12-14)

We probably have never scoured rust off a bronze ewer or worked with papyrus reeds. Still, the teaching is clear enough:

monastic authority should not function in a violent manner. That is good advice for any authority that wishes to maintain the respect of its subjects, but there may be even more at stake here. The quote of Isaiah 42.3 is from the First Servant Song and refers to the mysterious figure of the Servant of YHWH. Isaiah presents the Servant as a non-violent messiah who refrains from accomplishing his mission brutally. Indeed, he chooses to be killed rather than to kill to save the people. In the New Testament, the church invokes this verse as a type of Jesus himself (Matt 12:20). So monastic authority has a high ideal to attain.

January 6

If you have a quarrel with someone, make peace before sundown.
(RB 4.73)

Father Jerome was standing at the bulletin board one day when a voice just behind him said: "I resign from your committee!" Turning around, he saw the back of Father Ernest retreating down the hall. Since he had no idea why his confrere was angry, he decided to follow him and find out. But when he knocked on the door, Ernest would not let him into his room. Determined to pursue the issue and not let it fester, Jerome forced his way into the room and declared he was not leaving without an explanation. But Ernest was not forthcoming. Indeed, he upped the ante, declaring that he would henceforth have nothing whatsoever to do with Jerome, even though they were next-door neighbors. And so it was for the next twenty-five years. Ernest was sent on mission to a chaplaincy, and no word passed between the two. Jerome assumed things would stay like that until death, but they did not.

One day during retreat when Jerome was sitting alone in the common room, a voice close behind him said: "Let's bury the hatchet!" And when he turned around, he saw only the back of Ernest retreating across the room.

January 7

[The prioress] should strive more to be loved than to be feared.
(RB 64.15)

In our time, fear has a bad name; therefore we probably accept this dictum of Benedict (quoted from Augustine) at face value. As a general principle, it is true that love is a higher emotion than fear. At the close of his chapter on humility, Benedict quotes with approval the text of 1 John 4:18: "perfect love drives out fear" (NAB). Nevertheless, it is quite possible to misunderstand this kind of maxim and thereby undermine it. In fact, the full quote of Augustine (RA 7.3) reads: "Although both things are necessary, one should prefer to be loved rather than feared." Augustine may mean that different people need to be approached differently, but it could also mean something else: Some people have an inordinate need to be loved. This can prove to be a crippling fault in a superior, who sometimes must act in a manner that she knows will not be accepted by those she is trying to help. In fact, it can almost be taken as axiomatic that a superior will be hated by some of her subjects; anyone who cannot bear that prospect should not take on this role.

January 8

When someone first comes to the monastic life, she should not be allowed entrance too easily, but as the Apostle says, "Test whether the spirits be godly" [1 John 4.1]. (RB 58.1)

When monasteries are desperate for new recruits, who can risk turning away a newcomer? In the verses that follow, Benedict shows that he means business: the postulant is left knocking four or five days! But it must also be pointed out that he was repeating a literary cliché from an earlier time; whether *any* of the monks actually rebuffed aspirants is doubtful. That seems to pay too little attention to charity. Yet there is a deeper truth that cannot be avoided, namely, that the call comes from God and not merely from the will of the seeker. Furthermore, monastic life is by definition a hard road to trudge. That is because it must involve a confrontation with the person's deepest "issues," from which no one can shield her. The role of monastic initiation is not to lure candidates into our web, nor is it to bar the door to them. It is to offer them a fair trial at self-transformation.

January 9

As for the goods of the monastery . . . the abbot should assign brothers of reliable life and habits and entrust to them, as he sees fit, these objects to be cared for and collected. (RB 32.1-2)

This little chapter follows the chapter on the cellarer and is about the care of monastic goods, but it does not even mention the cellarer. Instead, the abbot is presented as the chief custodian of the goods, and he is admonished to take this role seriously.

There are at least two possible interpretations of this chapter. (1) It witnesses to a very early stage of Benedict's community when it was so small that one official could manage everything. (2) Goods are so important in Benedict's eyes that they warrant supervision by the top superior of the monastery. If the latter fork in the road is taken, it should not suggest that Benedict is a materialist. Rather, he should be seen as a holistic thinker who resists separating the physical and the spiritual. For him, the spiritual head of the monastery must involve himself at some level with the conditions of material life. Otherwise, they become "just things" and lie open to neglect or abuse.

January 10

We must constantly recall the commandments of God,
continually mulling over how hell burns sinners who despise God,
but for those who fear God there will be eternal life. (RB 7.11)

This ferocious verse, taken from the first step of humility, is exactly the kind of religious sentiment most people today no longer accept. And since Benedict has a general reputation of being gentle and moderate, they may be shocked to learn that it comes from him. Lest we suspect that "he just had a bad day," we should know that he expresses the same idea at least four times in the Rule. We have to accept that on some questions our religious sensibilities may be quite different from those of the ancient monks—and from our grandparents! That should warn us not to facilely read our own ideas into these texts. There is a gap between them and us. Yet it is still good for us to read them and ponder them, because they can cut through some of our self-absorption and complacency. And their tough doctrine of hell is based on the very modern idea that everyone has a right to choose one's own future. Is it for or against God?

January 11

And so, we have asked the Lord about dwelling in his tent, and we have received the rule for living there: to fulfill the duties of an inhabitant. (RB Prol. 39)

It is interesting that at least one very important RB manuscript ends the Prologue with this verse. "If we fulfill the duties of an inhabitant, we will be heirs of the kingdom of heaven." But one unfortunate implication of that version is to place the kingdom of heaven entirely on the other side of death. For the New Testament, however, the kingdom is already in our midst. Indeed, one could interpret the image of the Lord's "tent" in this verse to refer to the beginnings of his kingdom in this world. At any rate, Benedict wants to insist once more that we have no part in that kingdom unless we live lives of practical obedience to God: "the duties of an inhabitant." Mere habitation in this tent/kingdom is no guarantee of spiritual success: we must act like a true denizen of the kingdom. In a world where many people think skin color or family lineage or membership in some larger entity brings entitlement, this is a hard message to assimilate.

January 12

The Apostle says: "Don't you know that the patience of God leads you to repentance?" [Rom 2:4]. (RB Prol. 37)

To judge from the number of times it is used and the key positions that he gives it, patience is one of Benedict's most important monastic virtues. This is the first usage of it in the

Rule and the subject is noteworthy: God himself is patient! The patience of God in this verse is not just a general virtue, but it has the specific purpose of giving us the time to repent. Indeed, the Latin terms *patientia* and *penitentia* form a strong alliteration, making a phrase that is easy to memorize. The early Christians must have thought a lot about patience, since they had several words for it, each of them with a slightly different slant. The precise term here is *makrothumia*, the willingness to allow another person to develop and grow (Rom 2:4). We are also told that God's patience "leads" us to repentance, so Benedict does not see it as merely passive. The knowledge that God is giving us time should not produce complacency but a new resolve to change.

January 13

Listen, my son, to the instructions of your master. (RB Prol. 1)

Benedict addresses the person who seeks admission to his monastery in a rather challenging way. Far from seeking to ingratiate himself with the newcomer and thereby lure him into the fold, he presents himself straightforwardly as "the master." And he demands complete attention from the aspirant. Although this may seem somewhat overbearing to our less authoritarian age, it is in fact merely realistic. Anyone who wishes to undertake the monastic life, or any other life of serious spiritual striving, has to be ready to "listen." This means that one must be ready to put aside all of one's preconceived plans and self-evaluations in order to be directed by the spiritual wisdom of another. Especially at first, the seeker for true spiritual wisdom and progress has to be convinced that the greatest danger lies in self-deception and that the only way out of that particular trap is attentiveness to the wisdom of a more experienced spiritual guide. For his part, the spiritual master has to be ready to provide "instruction," even though this does not mean he knows everything or that he has nothing to learn from the seeker.

January 14

The brothers should offer their advice with all deference and humility, and not presume to assert their views in a bold manner. (RB 3.4)

The context here is the monastic chapter meeting. The brothers are invited to give their advice on a certain matter. For Benedict, it is important *how* they give that advice. They are to speak in a humble, not a bold manner. This may seem obvious for people who are dedicated to humility, but we live in an adversarial culture and people are accustomed to verbal combat at public meetings. In this matter, it would help a lot if the monk would keep in mind the basic dynamics of the monastic chapter meeting. He is asked for advice. He is not invited to persuade anybody, much less bully them. He knows that his bit of advice will merely be part of the mix that the abbot must sort through in the end. His job is not to prevail but to contribute to a true discernment of the will of God. Of course, these things are easier to say than they are to do. When people care passionately about an issue they will show it. The abbot must also take *that* into consideration.

January 15

So let us consider carefully how we should behave in the sight of God and all his angels. When we stand singing psalms, let our mind be in harmony with our voice. (RB 19.6-7)

This verse is part of an *a posteriori* argument that is employed in chapter 19 of the Rule: If God is present and alert to us everywhere, all the more so when we are praying the Divine Office. The reasoning has some cogency, since our prayer is specifically addressed to God. But some may find it a bit naive since God has no particular need of our prayers. The first five verses emphasize our fear of the Lord in response to God's omnipresence and surveillance. I remember an old book in the novitiate that depicted angels with wicker baskets picking up garbled words from monks reciting the Office in choir. The last verse is rather hard, since it seems to demand that we concentrate on every word we sing in the Office. If that is the intent, then it seems misguided since no one can keep up with the choir if she lingers on this word or that. Surely it is better to "go with the flow" and just trust that God hears us.

January 16

[The cellarer] should give the brothers their due portion of food without disrespect or delay that would upset them. He should remember the Lord's saying about the fate of anyone "who should upset one of these little ones" [Matt 18:6]. (RB 31.16)

It cannot be denied that the Benedictine cellarer has a good deal of power. The plain fact is that everybody in the monastery depends on him for their material needs. Of course, they are spared the worry about supplying their own needs, but they are also placed in a condition of extreme vulnerability. This means that the cellarer can take it for granted that the individual with whom he is dealing will be especially sensitive to the way he is being treated. In Benedict's language, the cellarer should avoid "upsetting" (saddening) the monks. Indeed, it might be said that community morale is just as important to the cellarer's work as are community goods. When people are treated with respect, they will put up with a good deal of hardship; but where it is lacking, they find it much harder to cope.

January 17

[Before Compline] someone should read from the Conferences *or the* Lives of the Fathers, *or something else that will uplift the hearers. But do not read the Heptateuch or the Books of Kings, for it will not be helpful to tired minds to listen to those books at that time of day. They should, though, be read at other times.* (RB 42.3-4)

In the days before the printing press made books relatively inexpensive, it was more practical to read aloud from the few books in the monastic library. In this case, there is public reading in the evening before Compline. Benedict suggests works from the collection of monastic writings, or else the Bible. But not just *any* books of the Bible! At that time of day, he thinks certain Old Testament books will not be uplifting, presumably because of their violence or their frank portrayal of sexuality. Still, Benedict is not exactly a prude. He does not mean that those books are to be altogether avoided—just in the evening. So we might call him a realist and an eminently practical man. It is helpful to know that Benedict does not let his ethical preoccupations override the objective basis of Christianity, namely, the whole Bible.

January 18

So then and there in the oratory she should be stripped of the clothes she is wearing and dressed in the garb of the monastery. (RB 58.26)

Although the early Christians were completely stripped at baptism, it is doubtful whether anyone ever was at reception into the novitiate. Still, the reception of a nun did feature a dramatic clothes-change in which the woman left the chapel in her street clothes and returned dressed in a wedding dress! We may wonder if that was appropriate, since the monastic habit did not figure in it. But in fact "the monastic habit" does not appear in this verse of RB either. The "garb of the monastery" simply means clothes belonging to the community, and not any specific symbolic garb. The point then is dispossession, not change of status. This is certain, because a couple of verses later Benedict insists that if she later wishes to leave the monastery, the "clothes of the monastery" should be taken off her before she departs. The whole thing sounds rather brutal, but it does show that these people were not playing games. When you entered monastic life, you left your other life behind you. You did not "sort of" become a monk.

January 19

Do not engage in empty babbling or joking. Do not engage in prolonged or explosive laughter. (RB 4.53-54)

Brother Bill was a great laugher; indeed, he was a tremendous laugher. When he laughed, the windows and the doors rattled. Brother Lawrence, on the other hand, was a quiet old man who spoke very slowly. Bill was sitting in the lunchroom one day regaling his cronies when Lawrence came in. "Well, Larry, how are ya?" he shouted. Larry began to carefully formulate an answer, but Bill paid no attention. He was on to the next joke, and soon had the whole crowd guffawing. The old man waited patiently to break in but could not find an opening when Bill or someone else was not raising a ruckus. Finally he found his chance. "You know, Bill," he said, "You ask a guy how he is and you don't even care about the answer." The whole place fell silent for about ten seconds.

January 20

After that she should live in the novice quarters, where they learn the Scriptures, eat and sleep. A senior should be assigned to them who is gifted in spiritual guidance and will look after them with careful attention. (RB 58.5-6)

Learn the Scriptures, eat and sleep. What an idyllic life! And it is to last for a full year. Before Vatican II, novices were often sequestered from the rest of the nuns. They had almost no social contacts with their family and little access to the mass media. It was the epitome of a sheltered life. For some reason, monasteries took these verses of the Rule almost literally. Was it wise to do so? In some ways, yes. To experience a sharp break with one's previous existence can be invigorating. It can also be gut wrenching. To have ample time to read and pray is a blessing at any time, but not all can appreciate it. The deep silence of the novitiate could be unnerving, but it did allow one's spiritual issues to surface. And one was not alone; there was a novice director who was at least theoretically capable of providing direction. Blessed the novice who had a director who was a true spiritual guide!

January 21

The abbot must keep an inventory so that as the brothers succeed one another in their assignments, he knows what he has given out and what he has gotten back. (RB 32.3)

Nowadays, the keeping of inventories and ledgers is usually the province of the cellarer, and it is considered a somewhat dreary task. But obviously it must be done if there is to be a rational management of the goods of the monastery. Far from a negligible function, some writers think that this was the indispensable foundation of modern economics, and that it may well have been the Benedictine monks who pioneered it. Some might consider this a feather in our cap, but others might wonder what all this has to do with the spiritual life and the kingdom of God?

Father Edgar was the kindest priest in the diocese. He gave away everything he had and was constantly in debt. So much so that the abbot had to bail him out again and again. Finally, he joined the military chaplaincy where they would make him keep to the budget—which suggests that some order is usually necessary to maintain charity for any length of time.

January 22

We can be sure that we are constantly observed by God from heaven, and that our deeds everywhere lie open to the divine gaze and are reported by the angels at every hour. (RB 7.13)

The notion that God is aware of every single thing we do is rather ambiguous. Fifty years ago it was a commonplace in

Catholic preaching. Apparently people found it inspiring and uplifting, but that may no longer be the case. One of the great Existentialist writers, Jean Paul Sartre, was outraged by the very idea that his privacy could be penetrated by anyone, even God. He said it was one of the reasons he simply could not believe in such a God. Since the drive for individual autonomy has become virtually epidemic in our culture, deep down we may feel the same. But before we get carried away, we should recall that the other side of the coin of privacy is abandonment. If we systematically exclude people from our lives, then we should not be surprised if there is nobody there when we need them. And the same goes for God. Do we or don't we wish to walk with God?

January 23

Therefore we must prepare our hearts and bodies to wage the battle of holy obedience to the commandments. (RB Prol. 40)

The term "hearts" here does not have a physical reference but a spiritual (or at least a mental) one. "Hearts and bodies" is a Hebraism for the whole human person, which is involved in the life of spiritual striving. Exactly how we prepare our bodies for holy obedience is not so obvious, but a text such as, "They have neither their bodies nor their wills at their disposal" (RB 33:4) shows that it was a typical expression. "Striving" is not seen primarily as the creative quest of the individual, but as submission to outside authority. This is characteristic of the Jewish view of faith. Mention of the "commandments" is certainly a sign that God is that authority, but the use of the monastic term "obedience" probably points ahead to the content of the Rule itself. Chapter 1 of the Rule shows that Benedict considers the cenobitic life to be a hard, even military, struggle.

The "battle," of course, is not against outside authority but against the forces of darkness, both inside and outside ourselves.

January 24

The loving Lord says: "It is not the death of the sinner that I want, but rather that he change his ways and live" [Ezek 33:11]. (RB Prol. 38)

In this verse of the Prologue, we do not have the usual perfunctory introduction: "The Lord says." Here the *loving* Lord speaks. The Latin term *pius* has a different connotation than our meaning of "devout." In this verse, and in the first verse as well, God is called *pius* because he has tender concern for his children, that is, the human race. This is at opposite poles from the ferocious theology that we sometimes hear ascribed to the God of the Jews! But in fact, it comes from a text of the Hebrew prophet Ezekiel. The grotesque idea that God somehow needs our suffering is quite foreign to the whole Bible and any interpretation that runs in that direction is essentially misinterpretation. Nevertheless, the Bible, and Benedict's Prologue, are realistic: each of us is a sinner that needs to repent and change her ways. Because he is "loving," we can be sure that God will promote that worthy project. In fact, without his grace, it is impossible.

January 25

Turn to [my instructions] with the ear of your heart. (RB Prol. 1)

The expression "ear of your heart" is a metaphor, for the heart does not literally have ears. What is more, Benedict may not mean exactly the same thing as we do by the word "heart." For us, the heart conjures up the symbols of Valentine's Day and has rather sentimental connotations. But for the ancient world, the heart is something else: the place of special encounter with God. As such, it is the center of spiritual attentiveness, the place where one heeds the voice of God. In this case, the voice is that of the monastic guide who will lead the postulant or novice. But for there to be any meaningful spiritual growth, the seeker must consider this to be the voice of God for him here and now. By his use of the term "heart," Benedict shows that this is not merely a matter of intellectual comprehension. Rather, it impacts the whole person, and it assumes total openness and good will. We have come to this "school of the Lord's service" (Prol. 45) to undertake the difficult process of self-transformation. We must strain with all our heart to hear and learn what will benefit us on that journey.

January 26

She should not be . . . jealous and suspicious; for then she will not find a moment's peace. (RB 64:16)

Abbot Ralph was not a suspicious man. In fact, he was trusting to a fault. Unlike his paranoid predecessor, Ralph would give you plenty of rope. If you chose to hang yourself with it, that was not his problem. But he had his limits. One day the phone rang in the dining room and the Abbot answered. "St. Placid's Abbey. Who do you want?" "Father Virgil." So the Abbot shouted at the crowd of monks eating lunch: "Virgil!" Someone hollered back: "He's in Alaska." The Abbot duly reported to the caller: "He's in Alaska." But then he stopped in his tracks. Alaska? Virgil had not asked him for permission to travel so far! In fact, he was not even aware that he was absent from his choir stall. The next day a sign appeared on the bulletin board: "Henceforth, anyone wishing to leave the lower forty-eight states must have my permission. Abbot Ralph."

January 27

Let all follow the guidance of the Rule, and no one should be so rash as to deviate from it in the slightest way. (RB 3.6)

Occurring as it does in the chapter on calling the brothers to counsel, Verse 3.6 of the Rule serves as a principle of equity for the whole community. As is well known, the Benedictine monastery is not a pure democracy. In fact, everything hinges on the guidance of the abbot. But such a benevolent dictatorship risks devolving into despotism unless it is counterbalanced by a Rule of Law. The crucial thing about such a Rule is that it is an objective standard apart from the personal opinions of any one person or party. In this case, it is clear that the abbot himself comes under the Rule. Moreover, the Rule exists as a body of rights as well as duties for every member of the community. Although the final sentence seems to make of the Rule almost a cult object, in fact the overall text of the Rule shows that Benedict allows a degree of flexibility in interpreting its provisions (see for example, RB 18.22).

January 28

When we wish to ask something of powerful people, we do not presume to do so except with humility and reverence. How much more should we petition our God, the Lord of the Universe, with great humility and total devotion. (RB 20.1-2)

When Benedict wishes to argue for reverence in prayer, he uses a bit of *a posteriori* reasoning to make his point: we do not approach the great ones of the earth carelessly; how much less the Lord of the Universe! A telltale word appears in this passage, namely, "presume." It might seem a throwaway but not for Benedict. He employs it over and over to describe a fundamental disruption in the proper order of things. Usually that means that a monk places himself on the same level as the abbot, but here the reference is more general. It is also theological, for lack of reverence before God, and especially in prayer, indicates a basic rejection of our creaturely dependence. We notice that humility is used twice in this passage, once as a synonym for reverence and again as a synonym for total devotion. This is very helpful, since it eliminates some of the distracting psychological overtones that are present in chapter 7, on humility.

January 29

[The cellarer] should give people what they need, and they should make their requests at the proper times. That way, no one will be aggravated or upset in the house of God. (RB 31.19)

Making requests at the proper times shows that the community respects the well-being of the cellarer and therefore avoids invading his privacy. Clearly, the cellarer is not "on duty" at all times. He is ready to respond to all emergencies but not to what are simply personal whims of the monks. To some extent he is a public figure who must expect to be approached at some inconvenient times. But he needs to maintain his personal integrity to the extent that he has some time to himself. In the previous verse, Benedict says that he should be given help. That should serve to divide up the responsibility so that one person will not be forever "on call." Those who cannot be bothered to observe the "right time" for transactions with the cellarer will have to be trained in these matters.

January 30

At the time for the Divine Office, as soon as he hears the signal the brother should drop whatever he has in hand and hurry with great haste . . . Thus, nothing should be put ahead of the Work of God. (RB 43.1, 3)

There is a charming story in monastic mythology of the monastic scribe who leaves a letter half-drawn to respond immediately to the signal for the Divine Office. Benedict is not quite so graphic or colorful, but the idea is the same: the call to prayer comes first. Anyone who has lived any length of time in a monastery knows that this principle can be costly, especially when one is engaged in very absorbing work that demands intense concentration. Yet, it is still possible to misinterpret these verses. They do *not* say that the Divine Office must be put ahead of every other form of monastic obedience! Some activities simply do not admit of interruption, even for prayer. If we insist on abandoning the printing press half through the run, or the cow giving birth, or the bread in the oven, we are asking for trouble. What Benedict means is that in ordinary circumstances, at prayer time one goes to pray.

January 31

If she has possessions, she should donate them to the poor beforehand,
or she should give them to the monastery by a formal donation.
She must not keep back anything at all for herself, for she knows that
henceforward she does not even have any more power over her own
body. (RB 58.24-25)

It is noteworthy how Benedict lays so much emphasis on
material dispossession in his chapter on monastic formation. It
almost suggests that he was used to receiving novices from
noble families who had many possessions. Indeed, medieval
monasteries admitted *only* such candidates, but they were not
required to divest themselves completely of their goods. That
was because the monasteries themselves were often so poor
they could not support their own members. The jarring remark
that one must put aside material goods since one does not even
have the disposal of one's own body should probably be construed to mean that the monastic will no longer make her own
life-decisions. Once a person has come to the point of that kind
of personal freedom, then it is no great sacrifice to surrender
material possessions.

February 1

Speak the truth in your heart and with your mouth. (RB 4.28)

Father Basil had been around a long time and he had a sharp
eye for what was wrong in the monastery. He was known to be
outspoken and he was rather proud of it. He seemed to be
courageous about controversial issues and so the monks often

voted him onto the Council of Seniors where he continued to be outspoken. Once, when he was on the Council of Seniors, the Abbot wrote a customary for the community and told the group to take it home and to write out their comments on it. This would be the first step in a long process of consultation and refinement. So the six councilors did as they were asked. Or at least five of them did. Then the Abbot collated their criticisms for everyone to see, which was rather remarkable since some of the criticisms were pungent. "Darn it," roared Basil, "if I had known that the rest of you guys were going to be so honest, I would have spoken my mind too!"

February 2

The decision should depend on the abbot's judgment, and everyone should go along with what he decides is beneficial for salvation. (RB 3.5)

Just as the arrangement of having the abbot make final decisions (with important exceptions) is not easy for the modern temper, even more so is the necessity for the monks to accept that decision. In a pure democracy, no decision is ever final; all is subject to review and contestation. But Benedict gives us a precious clue as to why this model is not appropriate in the monastic community. It is because things are being decided in a way that is "beneficial for salvation" *(salubrius)*. When we remember that, we find it easier to put aside personal agendas and party politics. Even though some people will find the decision more to their liking than others, this is not a contest in which there are winners and losers. The abbot has to make a final determination that promotes the salvation of *everybody*. Some may suspect that all of this is merely a cover for suffocating authority, but it is actually part of the logic of spiritual discernment.

February 3

One must note carefully whether the novice really seeks God, and whether she is eager for the Work of God, obedience and hardships. She should be told all the hard and harsh things that lead to God. (RB 58.7-8)

Perhaps we can understand why the novice must be drawn to the Divine Office, and why she must be docile to obedience. After all, those are a couple of the pillars of Benedictine spirituality. But what about "hardships"? Does that suggest a kind of spiritual boot camp? I doubt it. It is simple enough to make things hard for neophytes. That is what hazing is all about. It is not what monasticism is all about. It seems to me that what is meant here, or at least what is needed, is a spirit of candor in the novitiate where the novice is helped to confront her own special problems. They will not all be overcome in one year, but one should at least come to a better understanding of self. She should also be helped to understand that the other nuns also have problems that she will one day need to live with. There is no reason whatever to paper over these matters in the novitiate.

February 4

We especially urge that if any are displeased with this distribution of the psalms, they arrange them as they see fit. But whatever they do, they should see to it that the full number of 150 psalms is sung each week. (RB 18.22-23)

In the early 1970s, many Benedictine monasteries did something they had never done before: they dared to remodel Benedict's Divine Office. In doing so, they were simply taking advantage of a privilege that Benedict himself gives them in this verse. But it must admitted that most monasteries went further. They not only rearranged things, they reduced the number of psalms. This was not done under the table but with the full concurrence of the Congress of Abbots held in Rome but perhaps against Vatican wishes. What was the rationale that could have driven the monks to such a desperate expedient? Simply this: we decided that we need to pray less in order to pray better. We have only so much time. How can we pray properly within that time frame? Only by slowing down. How can we slow down? Only by reducing the number of psalms. You will find very few monks now who do not like the "new" Office.

February 5

As for self-will, we are forbidden to carry it out, for Scripture says to us: "Beware of your own desires" [Sir 18:30]. And so we ask God in prayer that his "will be done in us" [Matt 6:10]. (RB 7.19-20)

Too often commentators have jumped to the conclusion that the cenobitic project is to domesticate or even eliminate the will of the monk. This is indeed the teaching of the Rule of the Master, who proposes that God's will should *replace* our will *(Thema Pater)*. The implication is that the human will is a serious spiritual problem. In fact, the will is an indispensable human faculty, and any true spiritual growth must involve the strengthening of the will. In most languages, "self-will" means precisely a *diseased* will that seeks autonomy in all it does, without outside interference. The quote from Sirach 18:30 about "desire" suggests that for Benedict, the problem here is not discernment and choice as such, but headlong ambition that will brook no opposition. But the monk needs a strong will to overcome hard obstacles, and monastic humility should not undermine that will.

February 6

Let us pray the Lord to command the help of his grace to aid us in what we cannot accomplish by nature. (RB Prol. 41)

As before (RB Prol. 3-4), here Benedict follows a call to obedience from the individual with a prayer to God for the "help of his grace." But as with the earlier passage, this one can suggest a certain ambiguity. Is God brought in simply to "fill in the gaps" of what we cannot accomplish on our own? If so, it is not an adequate account of Christian grace, which insists that divine grace must be the primary energy for the beginning, middle and end of salvific human action. Psychologically speaking, the problem with this approach is that the more we can do for ourselves, the less we seem to need God. But true Christian faith realizes that we can do nothing at all without God's help; we cannot even *want* to do good without it. God is not just an afterthought or a nice addition to a pious life: in the realm of grace, God is *everything.* This is an Augustinian position that is not so easy to correlate with vigorous ascetic striving, but it is still our faith.

February 7

Willingly accept the advice of your devoted father. (RB Prol. 1)

"Willingly" seems to be a sort of truism, but it is by no means to be taken for granted. If the person is not ready to accept spiritual guidance from another, he should not present himself at the door of the monastery. Good will is of the essence. The "advice" of the guide will sometimes be a matter of obedience and therefore not leave much choice, but in fact one is always free to take it or leave it, to come or go. Although cenobitic monks are bound by obedience to the abbot, all true spiritual progress is a matter of free will. As for a "devoted" father, the word *pius* can also have the meaning of "loving." Indeed, it would appear that love between master and disciple is crucial to the spiritual life. This does not imply emotional attachment, but unless the seeker is convinced that the master desires nothing more than his deepest personal growth, it is hard to see how he can accept his teaching.

February 8

If there are less important decisions to be made concerning the affairs of the monastery, the abbot should consult only the seniors. For it is written: "Do everything with counsel, and afterward you will have nothing to regret" [Prov 31:3]. (RB 3.12-13)

This provision of chapter 3 of the Rule applied especially to large monasteries where it would be burdensome to gather the whole group for day-to-day decision making. In fact, modern monasteries *must* have a "council of seniors" that meets regularly and gives advice and consent on certain matters. Beyond these legal requirements, it is a matter of ordinary prudence for a leader to seek counsel for the decisions that must be made. In a system such as the Benedictine community, the abbot can decide many things without counsel if he prefers. But the text of Proverbs 31:3 indicates this tendency to go it alone may well result in "regret." Furthermore, it is not enough for the abbot to just go through the motions of convening advisors and letting them talk. Advisors can sense right away if the leader is really listening and whether he already has his mind made up. In that case, the tendency is for the counselors to allow the abbot to simply "swing in the wind."

February 9

We should petition our God, the Lord of the Universe, with great humility and total devotion. (RB 20.2)

Our ancestors left kings and princes behind in Europe, so why should we be attracted to a regal image of God? Nonetheless, we are also now aware of the utter immensity of the universe; if God is its Lord, then God is indeed Someone to be reverenced with humility and devotion. It is often said that the liturgical reforms of Vatican II have had the unfortunate side effect of decreasing the element of reverence and awe in the Church's worship. This need not be. Just because a good deal of fussy formality was set aside should not doom us to irreverence. We can maintain a truly reverent atmosphere of prayer in the Divine Office by means of simplicity and silence rather than pomp and circumstance. Humility and devotion in the Office can be promoted by external means, but they will never happen automatically. Only a reverential heart will pray the Office as it is meant to be prayed.

February 10

When the abbot has listened to the advice of the brothers, let him ponder the matter and then do what he thinks best. (RB 3.2)

St. Benedict's chapter meetings are not strictly democratic. Only the abbot can convene them; he sets the agenda and presents the issues. After the monks have given their opinions, no vote is taken and the abbot alone makes decision. Nowadays, the canon law of the Catholic Church requires that a vote of the community be taken on certain very important matters such as the reception of a new monk and the expenditure of large amounts of money. But aside from that, the process here in chapter 3 of the Rule is much like what takes place in any complex organization. Healthy leaders want to hear the honest opinions of their colleagues. They know full well that some of them will be contradictory, but that is to be expected. Someone must sift through this variety of options and make a choice. That someone, in this case the abbot, must be willing to make a decision and stand by it. He knows he may be wrong, but the only other option is majority rule and that is not in Benedict's plan.

February 11

If anyone arrives at Vigils after the Gloria of Psalm 94, he is not to take his own place in choir. That is why we want that psalm said slowly and with pauses. (RB 43.3-4)

St. Benedict is certainly one of those people for whom tardiness is a serious problem, which is why he devotes a considerable chapter to curing it. There is an objective reason for not coming late to the Divine Office: it causes disruption and it is a symbol of lack of zeal for the house of God. Besides that, some people simply cannot stand tardiness, either in themselves or in others. They are promptness fanatics. Benedict is probably not in that category, since he goes out of his way *not* to punish latecomers, at least to the Night Office. To give them an extra chance to arrive on time, he wants the opening psalm (94 [95]) said very slowly. If he wanted to be vindictive, he would not have made this kind of concession. It might be added that it is a rare monastery that does not suffer from at least a few latecomers, and some of these are otherwise exemplary monks.

February 12

The whole community should answer this verse three times, adding the Gloria Patri at the end. Then the sister novice should prostrate at the feet of each one, asking for their prayers. And from that day onward, she should be considered a member of the community. (RB 58.22-23)

It is only fitting that the monastic community should take an active part in the most crucial part of the profession ceremony. When the novice has sung her *Suscipe* ("Receive me . . . ") the community repeats the words. In doing this, the rest of the sisters are renewing their own profession. Besides doing that, they are also receiving the novice into their midst as a full-fledged member. In the Rule, this is symbolized by the prostration of the sister before each member. Nowadays, however, each member bestows the kiss of peace on the novice, which seems like a clearer symbol. In fact, the modern profession ceremony includes many things that do not appear in the Rule of St. Benedict. It is perhaps not so important that our practice concur with the Rule in all details, but we must certainly do so in essentials. And one of those essentials is that profession symbolize acceptance by the whole community.

February 13

Obey the abbot's orders in all things, even if he—God forbid!—acts otherwise. Remember the Lord's command: Do what they say, not what they do. (RB 4.61)

The whole juniorate (monastics in temporary profession) was in a flutter because the junior-master, Father Ansgar, was to give a conference. It was his first conference, and everyone was fascinated by the prospect. When he was appointed the previous week by the abbot, someone remarked that he was perhaps the least likely person in the whole monastery to be assigned to such a job. For Ansgar was an irregular monk. Unlike the other, ordinary monks, he was unable to manage such elementary matters as coming to meals and choir, or at least coming on time. Indeed, his *horarium* (schedule) did not seem to coincide with that of anyone else in the place. He might be seen at 3 a.m. walking down the hall in his bathing suit, dragging a long rope. He lived at the lake all summer, more or less reverting to nature. As for his room, it was a jumble of all things, living and dead. The big question was how he would be able to demand order of anyone else? As it turned out, the conference that evening was very short, consisting of one sentence. As he gazed intently on his new charges, Ansgar said in his soft, quavering voice: "Do not do what I do; do what I say."

February 14

She should "not be restless" [Isa 42:4] and troubled, extreme and bullheaded, not jealous and suspicious; for then she will not find a moment's peace. (RB 64.16)

This list of six character defects to be avoided in a superior is anchored in the First Servant Song of Isaiah. It is responsible exegesis to use the magnificent theology of Isaiah as the basis for abbatial authority. This is the case in the New Testament, which several times points to the Servant Songs as a key to understanding the nonviolent ethos of Jesus. On the psychological level, it can be noted that most of the traits listed here are not just faults not to be committed but fundamental character defects that would make it very difficult to exercise monastic authority. This is not an absolute principle, since there have certainly been great leaders who have suffered from some of these faults (for example, the paranoia of Douglas MacArthur). The question is: what causes these negative feelings and reactions? If the cause is a deep doubt of one's own personal worth, this can effectively undermine any meaningful authority. A Christian superior must be convinced first of all that she is loved by God.

February 15

The one to be received must first promise stability, fidelity to the monastic lifestyle and obedience before all in the monastery. This is done before God and his saints, so she should know that if she ever goes back on it, she will be condemned by the One whom she mocks. (RB 58.17-18)

In these verses, Benedict speaks of monastic profession and the promises that nuns make. That may surprise some people: what ever happened to poverty, chastity and obedience? Those are in fact implied in the ancient Benedictine formula. Indeed, analysis of the complex literary tradition that lies behind this chapter shows that for Benedict, stability, fidelity to the monastic lifestyle and obedience were really just parts of one intention: to be a good monk. From what he adds, it is obvious that Benedict does not take these matters lightly. We make our promises before God, and it is he whom we offend if we do not hold fast to them. But the church in our day does not believe that it is useful to try to hold people to values that they no longer can or will maintain. And surely the monastic community has no business acting as the scourge of God on a member who leaves.

February 16

If a sister meets or sees guests, she should humbly greet them, as we said. Then she should beg a blessing and move on, explaining that she is not permitted to converse with a guest. (RB 53.24)

We do not observe this regulation, and it is questionable if most of us believe it. Why not simply expunge it from the text? Because one does not do that to classic documents. And besides, the verse is *not* sheer nonsense. There are monks and nuns who should not spend a lot of time with guests. They are looking for a welcome ear or a shoulder to cry on, but that is not why guests come to the monastery. In the *Life of Pachomius* (G1 40), a local priest is indignant that the guesthouse is built outside the monastic compound. Pachomius says in effect: "Look, we have some pretty rough types around here. I don't want them bothering the guests!" Still, there is something stiff and unnatural about keeping the community and the guests completely apart. If the guest wants to consult a monk or a nun, someone should be available. And if they meet casually, charity dictates a pleasant interchange.

February 17

With good reason we learn to steer clear of pursuing our own will, for we dread the warning of Holy Scripture: "There are paths that seem straight to us, but ultimately they plunge into the depths of hell" [Prov 16:25]. (RB 7.21)

In a sense, we cannot avoid "pursuing our own will," if that refers to a life of adult responsibility. But the biblical text that Benedict quotes shows that he is thinking of a particular problem in regard to the will. The verse from Proverbs is talking about self-deception, which is the occupational hazard of all who possess a personal inner life. One of the most serious problems of the spiritual life is how to escape from the prison of mirrors that is the self. One remedy is to give oneself over to a personal spiritual guide. In the world of the cenobium (monastic community), there is the added figure of the abbot, who is the official representative of the community and to whom each monk is bound in obedience. For one who is looking for an objective point of reference and a way out of self-deception, even an unsympathetic abbot can be of great value.

February 18

And if we wish to flee the punishment of hell and attain everlasting life, while there is still time and we are in this body, and there remains time to accomplish all these things in the light of this life, we must run and accomplish now what will profit us for eternity. (RB Prol. 42-44)

This is a particularly full, and even prolix, expression of an idea that is expressed several times in the Prologue: Time is short and we must use it to change our ways and prepare for the Last Judgment. The source, which is the author of the Rule of the Master, has used many elements to stress the fleeting nature of earthly time and especially of *our* time on earth. Benedict will speak often of "running," but this is headlong flight, a mad dash for safety from impending doom. Although death is not mentioned as such, it is the obvious antithesis of "everlasting life" and "eternity"—or it is implied in the expression "light of this life," for once the light is extinguished, darkness prevails. As always in the Prologue, our response to this impending danger is action: "we must accomplish" (twice). The listener is not encouraged to panic, which can be a cause of paralysis but rather to swing into purposeful action.

February 19

Put it into action! (RB Prol. 1)

Although the first verse of the Prologue begins with receptivity ("listen," "turn to," "accept"), the climax has to do with implementation. Granted, there is a contemplative stance of openness that must come first; nevertheless, the spiritual life is not exclusively passive. One is expected to do something! This seems to be especially true of the monastic way of life, which definitely involves a concrete lifestyle. From its earliest beginnings, the monastic life has required certain choices and behaviors. For example, the most universal monastic "practice" is celibacy: monks do not marry. Although there are many other monastic practices that can be argued about, what is beyond discussion is the practical nature of the enterprise itself: monasticism demands action. This may make it harder for our own age than for previous ones, because we are used to a variety of options, often ending in no choice at all. And we hesitate to close off alternate possibilities in favor of one lifestyle. For Benedict, however, monasticism is not just one interesting idea among many in the panoply of human philosophies. It is a concrete way of life that demands action.

February 20

"What are the Tools of Good Works?" First, "to love the Lord God with all your heart, all your mind and all your strength" [Mark 12:30], then "your neighbor as yourself" [Mark 12:31]. Then "not to kill, not to commit adultery, not to steal, not to covet, not to give false testimony" [Matt 19:18-19], to honor everyone, "not to do to another what you do not want done to yourself" [Matt 7:12]. (RB 4.1-9)

Someone glancing at the beginning of this famous chapter for the first time might wonder why it is addressed to monks. Haven't they long ago mastered these elementary Jewish and Christian principles? Apparently not in the opinion of Benedict! As a matter of fact, no one ever moves beyond the point where these foundations are irrelevant to him. Of course, we do not expect monks to be tempted to kill each other (though some have actually done so!) but that is not the point. We are first of all Christians and only second are we monks. Although modern monasticism is usually rather closely tied to the Church, it was not always so. Some monks regarded themselves as "super-Christians" and that always signaled the start of trouble. Most of all, the commandment to love God and love neighbor (see Mark 12:29-31) must remain the core of every Christian monastic philosophy. Apart from that we risk becoming a strange aberration, useless to God and to human beings.

February 21

Let us also know that we shall make ourselves heard [in prayer], not with many words, but with purity of heart and tearful compunction. (RB 20.3)

The original inspiration for this verse is probably Matt 6:7, which criticizes wordy prayers that seem to assume that God is deaf or needs to be persuaded. It would seem that the point here is different. The contrast is between verbosity and intensity. Purity of heart is an ancient concept that can easily be misunderstood. The reference is not to sexual chastity but to focus versus dispersion. In this way of thinking, the impure heart is one that is dissipated with overstimulation and a plethora of desires. The pure heart has but one focus and that is God. Still, this is not simply a matter of concentration. Some disciplined, powerful intellects still do not know how to pray. What they may lack is depth of conviction and feeling, represented here by the idea of tearful compunction. This expression does not imply a morbid spirituality but rather a heart that is not "hard" or "hard-bitten." Benedict says more about prayer than he is often given credit for.

February 22

The sick are to be cared for before and above all else, for Christ is truly served in them. He himself said: "I was sick and you visited me" and "Whatever you did to these little ones, you did to me" [Matt 25:36, 40]. (RB 36.1-3)

For Benedict, opening statements are important, so many of his chapters begin with a memorable saying. And in a few instances, he uses a famous biblical verse to lead off his treatise. In this case, he brings forward two sayings on the care of the sick from the famous Last Judgment scene of Matthew 25. In that chapter, the sheep and the goats are accepted or rejected on the grounds of practical charity. In both cases, they are surprised at the verdict, since they did not suspect that it was Jesus himself whom they were aiding or neglecting. The remarkable thing about Matthew 25 is that it does not seem to be about "religion" at all. There is no talk about saying our prayers or performing our devotions. And the truly astonishing element of the chapter lies in the claim that in helping the needy, one is encountering Jesus himself.

February 23

We have decided they must stand in the last place or apart so they will reform because of the shame of being seen by all. (RB 43.7)

This verse refers to latecomers to the Divine Office. Unlike many first-class theaters, Benedict does not lock the doors once the play starts until the first intermission. He wants the monks to come into the oratory, but they must go to a special place in order to atone for their fault of coming late. How are they punished? Simply by being seen by others. This is what "shame" means in traditional culture: one is publicly exposed to the accusatory gaze of others. In our culture, that would not be so burdensome, but in Mediterranean society it has always been the worst kind of suffering. Until about 1970, most American monasteries still asked members who arrived late for Office to "kneel out" in the middle of the sanctuary for a few moments. This was a strictly perfunctory practice, with no connotation of blame. Neither does Benedict distinguish between necessary and gratuitous tardiness. Perhaps that is why the custom finally disappeared.

February 24

"Receive me, Lord, as you have promised and I shall live. And do not dash my hopes" [Ps 118(119):116]. (RB 58.21)

I would like to quote the great Italian commentator, Anselmo Lentini, on this verse: "With his hands raised in the prayer position, his heart full of love and generosity, in the ineffable sentiment of feeling himself outside and above the whole world where he can be with the God of his heart, the novice prays that God will accept his total self-dedication. He is sure of the favor, the engagement, the fidelity of God, who at that moment embraces him with tender affection. And there is no monk who does not feel his soul renewed with fresh joy and moving sweetness at the memory of his own *Suscipe*" (p. 526). Besides being a wonderful piece of spiritual rhetoric, this comment locates the center of monastic vows where it belongs—on God. Whatever else takes place in such a ceremony, it is essentially a covenant between the individual and God. That is why the central prayer of the ceremony begs God to grant the petitioner what He himself has promised, namely, eventual union with God Himself.

February 25

Long for eternal life with the desire of the Spirit. (RB 4.46)

Father Daniel was worried. Although the first years of his monastic life had been hard ones, with uncongenial, suspicious superiors, he now had an abbot who loved him. And he loved the abbot in return. But that was the problem, because the abbot seemed to let him do anything he pleased. In itself, that was pleasant enough, but it still worried Dan because it flew in the face of the whole monastic ideology. He knew that Benedict puts a high premium on prompt obedience and frowns on self-will. "They prefer to walk according to the judgment and command of another, living in cenobitic community with an abbot over them" (RB 5.12). And he knew that this philosophy often requires that the monk abandon his own plans and fall in with the plans of others. So one day Dan marched into the Abbot Richard's office and said: "You know, I'm uneasy." "Why so, Dan?" "Because you let me do anything I want." The abbot sat there for a few moments chewing his pencil. "As I see it," he said, "the real question is whether you want what you ought to want."

February 26

When she has managed her office well, the prioress will hear from the Lord what that good servant heard who distributed grain to his fellow servants promptly: "Yes, I tell you, he will set him over his whole estate" [Matt 24:47]. (RB 64.21-22)

Since few of us have ever had direct experience of the world of the *latifundia,* large estates managed for absentee owners, this imagery might be a bit confusing. The reference is to a manager who represents the owner in his absence, but who must never usurp the owner's prerogatives. Of course, as other parables make clear, owners want profits. If the steward cannot show them, he will be in trouble. In fact, the steward had a difficult job, and it is hard to be sympathetic toward these absentee landowners. Still, Benedict focuses on the responsibility of the steward to take good care of his fellow servants. That is certainly the basic charge of the Benedictine abbot or prioress whose chief aim is not to improve the financial bottom-line of the monastery. Remember also that the landowner here is not a hard-bitten millionaire but the ever-loving God.

February 27

The clothing taken off [the novice] should be placed in the wardrobe for safekeeping. If he should ever agree to the devil's suggestion that he should leave the monastic life—and may it never happen!—then the clothes of the monastery should be stripped off him before he is turned out. (RB 58.27-28)

These are hard verses, not because they are unclear but because they are perfectly transparent. Clothes are being used here to reinforce membership and obligation. Notice that the habit is not so much to symbolize this or that spiritual truth; rather they are the "clothes of the monastery." They are GI, government issue. But they are also a sign of belonging. It is hard to get into Benedict's monastery, and it is hard to get out. If someone should ever get such a strange idea (to leave), then all hell breaks loose. Before he can leave on his own, he is "turned out." This kind of thinking perdured in our monasteries until Vatican II. Today, if someone wishes to depart, they do so with our blessing and good will. But have we also lost a sense of the sacredness of vows, of belonging? I should hope not.

February 28

[The monks] should not consider anything personal property, absolutely nothing, no book, no writing tablet, no stylus: absolutely nothing.
(RB 33.3)

At first blush, someone might get the impression that the "lady doth protest too loudly!" But it is possible that this verse was written in reply to those monks who question his doctrine that monastic dispossession ought to be absolute. As a completely practical matter, they are right. People always will have some items that only they use. The old monastic joke about "our handkerchief" is not completely without point. From the psychological point of view, one wonders if anyone can function without some little corner to call her own? Still, in our age of individualism and consumerism, the doctrine of dispossession could serve as a healthy corrective to mindless accumulation. There is something unseemly about a monastic cell (private room) piled high with "stuff." That does not prove conclusively that the inhabitant is in violation of RB 33, but it is hard to see how she is not.

February 29

We should be convinced that our carnal drives are well known to God, for the Prophet says to the Lord: "All my desire is before you" [Ps 37(38):9]. (RB 7.23)

All through the last part of the first step of humility, Benedict fluctuates between "desire" *(voluptas)* and "will" *(voluntas).* Since the Latin words are so close in spelling, it is quite possible that the scribes sometimes made mistakes. On first blush, it seems that there is a big difference between the two realities, but that may not be so. For one thing, *desideria* does not refer to sensuality as such, but rather to *misplaced* desires, much in the same way as "flesh" (Greek, *sarx*) in the writings of Paul. Furthermore, although we find it hard to admit it, our "will" in some matters is less a matter of rational choice than irrational drives. Or at least we are often driven by feeling rather than ideas. Both are good, but they are not the same thing. Sometimes we are the last ones to understand our own motivation, but we can be sure that God understands.

March 1

Therefore we must establish a school for the Lord's service. (RB Prol. 45)

This is one of the most often quoted texts in the Rule of St. Benedict, but it really is from the Rule of the Master. Since Benedict often alters the teaching of the Master, we might ask how he does so here. A short answer can be had by skipping directly to RB Prol. 50, which is the very next verse in the RM. In his view, in the school of the Lord's service what we learn is suffering. This is no doubt true, but Benedict has seen fit to insert four verses of material between these two poles (vv. 45 and 50), and these verses sharply change the meaning. Apparently for Benedict, the monastic school is also a place where we learn to *enjoy God* and right now, not just in a heavenly future as the Master teaches. What is more, the term "school" *(schola)* has that kind of potential, for the Greek, *skole,* refers precisely to leisure and contemplation! That may seem a bit of a "stretch," but it helps to unpack a dense phrase like "the school for the Lord's service."

March 2

You will return by the labor of obedience to the one from whom you became estranged through the carelessness of disobedience. (RB Prol. 2)

The second verse of the Prologue relies on theology strictly speaking, for it is clearly a reference to God. Since the hearer is a newcomer, she cannot be accused of disobedience to the prioress (master), so the reference must be to God. To tell the neophyte that she is "estranged" from God may seem unduly harsh, but it seems that Benedict wants to lay the cards on the table from the beginning: the novice is a sinner. Of course, we are all sinners, but it is assumed that monastic veterans know very well that they are sinners. In contrast, the newcomer may not be aware of this problem, or at least not think it is a pressing one. But for Benedict, it is *the* basic problem that must be addressed by a serious monastic life. One especially salutary effect of this blunt approach is to make sure we understand that monasticism is not some kind of nice addition to a Christian life; it is an intense form of that life itself.

March 3

Deny yourself in order to follow Christ [Matt 16:24]. Chastise your body [1 Cor 9:27]. Do not be pleasure-loving, but love fasting. Assist the poor, clothe the naked. Visit the sick, bury the dead [Matt 25:36]. Help those in trouble, console the sorrowful. (RB 4.10-19)

This block of verses from chapter 4, "The Tools of Good Works," is something of an arbitrary collection, yet it also has its own logic. Someone has pointed out that this chapter tends to alternate between asceticism and practical charity. The introduction further yokes them to the following of Christ. Although the idea of following Christ is fundamental to the Gospels, we must remember that it is by way of the Cross. That does not mean we go looking for ways to suffer, but it does surely mean that we attempt to live out the corporal works of mercy found in Matthew 25, the Last Judgment. But where does asceticism come in? When we actually try to do some good to others, we soon find out that we are shackled by our own selfishness. To avoid self-indulgence ought to help to free us from this kind of crippling self-concern. By extension the monastic community, which is supposed to practice systematic asceticism, should be thereby bolstered to serve the weak and the poor who come to it for help.

March 4

The sick brothers should be given a separate room and an attendant who is God-fearing, devoted and careful. (RB 36.7)

To give the sick a special room and a special attendant was a first in monastic history and perhaps the true beginning of modern hospital practice. But we might wonder a bit about Benedict's qualifications for the nurse. Nowadays we want our nurses to be registered nurses; for him it was more important that they be "God-fearing, devoted and careful." Of these, the first is perhaps most evocative, for it summarizes his whole view of Christian monastic interrelations. Why must the nurse be God-fearing? Simply because God/Christ is particularly present in the sick monk. That is the teaching contained in Matthew 25, which is the biblical basis for the first part of this chapter on the sick. Since the sick are weak and marginalized, it is a temptation to give them less than our full attention. For

Benedict, this would be a serious spiritual mistake. What is more, Benedict's God is rather formidable; to ignore God in the sick person is to court disaster.

March 5

Should anyone neglect the goods of the monastery or fail to keep them clean, he shall be reprimanded. If he does not improve, he is to suffer the discipline of the Rule. (RB 32.4-5)

Although the reference here seems general, the title of chapter 32 shows that the goods in question are in fact tools *(instrumenta)* and even more specifically *iron* tools. At the time of Benedict, iron tools were not as common or cheap as they are now. They were precious and rather rare, so much so that any neglect of them was a serious breach of monastic poverty. When an iron tool is not kept clean, it rusts. What is more typical of the American countryside than farmsteads full of rusting junk? Perhaps this is unavoidable, but from what we can tell, it would drive Benedict to distraction. In the sixth century, there were no landfills full of rusting junk! Further, it is typical of a modern commune that the tools are poorly maintained and quickly deteriorate. Why? Because they belong to "nobody." Or at least nobody thinks they are his personal responsibility. Again, Benedict cannot accept that kind of attitude.

March 6

If they were to remain outside (during the Office), some of them might go back to bed and sleep. Or some might sit down and gossip, "giving

the devil an opening" [Eph 4:27]. They should come inside; that way
they will not lose everything and they will improve for the future.
(RB 43.8-9)

Tardiness seems to be an occupational hazard for monks.
Perhaps because they go to church so often, some of them find
it very hard to tear themselves away from what they are doing
(sometimes sleeping!) to get there on time. Other monks are
much more punctilious, and the latecomers vex them no end.
They may be tempted to close and bolt the doors once and for
all, teaching the sluggards a lesson they will not forget. Benedict does not like tardiness, but he avoids this kind of drastic
response. He does so because he suspects that it will simply
make the problem worse. Maybe he is heeding the old principle that "the best is the enemy of the good." Although he
does not say so in so many words, it looks like Benedict feels
that simply being present for the Office will help to heal the
situation.

March 7

She should make a written document of her promise in the name of the
saints whose relics are there, and the name of the current prioress.
She should write her petition with her own hand, or if she is illiterate,
she may surely ask someone else to write it for her. Then the novice
signs it and personally lays it on the altar. (RB 58.19-20)

The profession of a nun is the most solemn thing she will
ever do, and Benedict spells out all its details so as to leave
nothing to chance. In an age when few people could write, he
insists that the petition be made in writing. In the years after
Vatican II, it became fashionable in some monasteries to allow
individuals to concoct the wording of their own charter. That

could result in some inspiring statements, but it could also descend into sentimental mishmash. Today we have returned to a standard profession formula, for this is a formal act controlled by the community. Most importantly, it is total offering of self that is symbolized by its connection with the altar on which the Holy Sacrifice of Christ's whole life (the Mass) will soon be offered.

March 8

Above all else, he should have humility. When he has no material goods to give someone who asks, at least he should return a kind word. For it stands written: "A good word is better than the best gift" [Sir 18:17]. (RB 31.13-14)

Cellarers live in different times. In one age, the monastery is in a period of prosperity and there is plenty to distribute where it is needed. But in another age, there may be barely enough to go around—or just plain poverty. A certain kind of personality will find it especially galling to have little or nothing to give to someone who obviously is in need. Benedict calls this "humility," and although that may seem an odd use of that word, it need not be. For some, the temptation will be to get defensive, complaining about conditions that no one can be blamed for. But Benedict suggests that no matter how empty the chest might be, there is still a good word to be had. When people do not receive what they think they need, they are in a particularly sensitive position and not to be further mauled with harsh words. Kindness costs nothing.

March 9

If she does not deserve expulsion, then not only should her petition to join the community be accepted, she should even be urged to stay so that others can learn from her example. After all, wherever we are, we are slaves of the same Lord and soldiers of the same King. (RB 61.8-10)

Benedict is quite open to learning from others. In this context, he recommends openness toward visiting nuns from afar, probably because through them one could well glimpse some fresh ideas. This is quite different from the typical attitude of those who live a ghetto existence. They carefully close themselves off from foreign sources of information and ideas. That requires a careful sealing off of all kinds of threatening ideas that could threaten local "orthodoxy." This kind of stance finds the modern world increasingly problematic, for if anything characterizes that world, it is the pervasiveness of mass communication. It is becoming harder and harder to isolate a population from these ideas, although totalitarian governments are trying their level best to do so. When a Benedictine superior thinks she must behave that way, she stands in violation of chapter 61.

March 10

Let [the abbot] tailor his approach to each one's character and understanding. That way he will suffer no loss of the sheep entrusted to him, but even enjoy the increase of a good flock. (RB 2.32)

"That will come to $37,470" said Abbot Leander. "Huh?" said Father Charles. He had just asked to take a trip to California to see his relatives, whom he never visited before. When the Abbot asked for the price tag, he admitted that it would cost $500, or about twice as much as was allowed for vacations in the new customary. Hearing this, Abbot Leander crunched some numbers on his pocket calculator and came up with $37,470. "What does that mean?" gasped Charles. "That's what it would cost if each monk went to California," said the abbot. Faced with this astounding feat of bookkeeping, Charles teetered between rage and despair. Without saying another word, he backed out the door, leaving Leander to contemplate his stalwart defense of the customary. It was his own creation and he was very proud of it, for he hoped it would give him firm guidelines for handling just this kind of irritating request. The next year, precisely to the day, Charles again showed up in the abbot's office. Before he got a word out, the abbot said "Alright, go to California."

March 11

[The nuns] may not consider even their own bodies or their wills at their own disposal. (RB 33.4)

This verse seems to run directly contrary to the deepest principles of human rights as understood by most contemporary thinkers (including the popes). In an important sense they are right, and monks are no exception to the rule. They, too, have an absolute personal integrity that no religious authority can or should violate. Of course, no superior would think of disregarding the bodily privacy of a subject, but some of them have less respect for the will of the individual. So then what does the verse mean? Scholars like J. Gribomont think that lying behind surface of this verse is the thought of St. Basil, one of Benedict's mentors: Since Christ gave his very life for the salvation of us all, a true disciple of Christ will do so for the Body of Christ (the community). Now, if one has committed her very self to the love of Christ and neighbor, why would she hold back any possession from them? (Long Rules 7.4, 9). Notice that "bodies and wills" is interpreted here to mean "very self."

March 12

The second step of humility is . . . to pattern our behavior on that saying of the Lord: "I have not come to do my own will but the will of the one who sent me" [John 6:38]. (RB 7.31-32)

Since it is easy to garble the question of the will, we have to tread very carefully here. According to Basil, whose influence is very strong over this part of the Rule, anyone who sets out to do the will of God will inevitably have to thwart his own will (Latin Rule 12). Notice that Basil does not tell us to set out to thwart our own will, as if that were the primary task of the monk. Many traditional monastic commentators seem to say just that. No, the task of the monk, like that of any truly religious person, is to find and do the will of God. But, according to Basil, we should not be surprised to find that the will of God for us is diametrically opposed to our own will. The Catholic belief in original sin says that the human will is often confused and disordered. Sometimes it is downright perverse.

March 13

Therefore we must establish a school for the Lord's service. (RB Prol. 45)

The Latin term *schola* has a far greater range of meaning than our "school" as an educational establishment. For example, any group organized for a given purpose was a "school" for them. But what is the purpose of a cenobitic monastery? Many have claimed that it is to produce saints, or even holy hermits! But others object, and rightly I think, that community as such has no purpose outside of itself. Although some people do not like to think about it, the Bible does in fact describe heaven as a communal experience (see Rev 14). In theological terms, we can say that monastic community is a foretaste of the heavenly community. That is a preposterous idea to contemplate on those days when confreres seem determined to drive us mad, but it is still theologically valid. To stay within the parameters of this famous verse: since the Lord is at the heart of the community, we serve the Lord precisely by serving the community.

March 14

The labor of obedience . . . the sloth of disobedience. (RB Prol. 2)

This may seem to be strange terminology, but we should remember that the subject really is sin and not just obedience. In the context of the Prologue, which urges the hearer to rise up and undertake the monastic life, "sloth" is more understandable. But the claim here is that all sin is "sloth," a refusal to exert oneself on the spiritual path. Or perhaps it even implies lagging behind God, who is forever moving on. At any rate, the opposite of spiritual sloth is here termed "labor." Benedict makes no secret of the fact that anyone who undertakes the monastic life is in for hard work, not a joy ride. All the more so as to conversion from sin, which demands all the energy we can muster. Of course it demands the grace of God, but that is not the emphasis in this verse. Throughout the centuries, the only respectable monastic life has been a strenuous one. It is not enough to simply "go with the flow," which too often leads in the wrong direction. At least in its beginnings, every monastic life will have to be a struggle. We are never simply "monks by nature."

March 15

Distance yourself from the ways of the world. Prefer nothing to the love of Christ. Do not carry out angry impulses. Do not wait for vengeance. Do not plot deceit. Do not give a false peace. Do not abandon charity. Do not swear oaths for fear of swearing falsely. Speak the truth both in your heart and with your mouth. (RB 4.20-28)

Despite the first verse, Benedict exhibits very little fear or hatred of "the world" such as we find in the Rule of the Master. It seems very important here to yoke this verse with the next one concerning the love of Christ. But note that this verse too is ambiguous. Does it refer to our love for Christ or to his love for us? Probably the latter, for it is precisely Christ's love for us, manifested in his death on a cross, that makes it at all possible for us to live out the ethic detailed in the verses that follow. As with many of the admonitions in the Prologue and the rest of chapter 4, many of the sins listed here seem to be characteristic of a close-knit, almost tribal, society. That is what a Benedictine monastery really is, a sort of Christian village or *ecclesiola* (little church) where people absolutely must learn to live by a higher ethic than what prevails in the world around them.

March 16

The kind of people with whom the abbot can confidently share his burden should be chosen deans. They should not be chosen for their rank, but for the merit of their lives and the wisdom of their teaching. (RB 21.3-4)

Most modern monasteries do not have deans, but the ideas expressed here can be applied to all communities. First, abbots and prioresses need to share their burdens. Even if the community is small and the workload is not heavy, it is not good for a religious superior to be alone. One of the occupational dangers of that position is isolation from the body of the group. This can create a gap of understanding and even generate unwarranted suspicion on all sides. Sharing the burden of office does not just mean delegation. It also includes the opportunity for mutual support of a fairly intimate kind. Benedict's deans are not mere functionaries. They are people of real wisdom, capable of genuine spiritual leadership. This means that the Benedictine monastery is not a "one-man-show," where a guru is surrounded by disciples. Authority here is shared as broadly as possible, and spiritual leadership is constantly being fostered in many persons.

March 17

This vice in particular should be ripped out by the roots, namely, that anyone would presume to give or receive anything without the permission of the abbot. (RB 33.1-2)

Chapter 33, "Whether Monks Should Consider Anything Their Own" has been called one of the harshest chapters in the whole Rule (A. de Vogüé), and this might be its toughest verse. The language is clearly violent: "ripped out by the roots" *(radicitus amputandum est),* and we might wonder whether that is justified, given the content of the chapter. Is private property such an evil vice? Certainly it isn't for our capitalist society, and the church generally promotes private property as a basic right of humanity. But the monastic cenobium is not just any society, and monks with a vow of poverty hold all things in common. What is more, Benedict seems to have gotten some of his ideas on this subject from John Cassian, who had a particular theory about avarice: it needs to be *completely* eradicated or it keeps coming back like a noxious weed. In addition, Benedict wants to eliminate "giving and receiving" from the monk's range of choices. That is the abbot's job, nobody else's.

March 18

If someone does not arrive at table before the verse so that all might say the verse together and pray and sit down to table as one . . . he should be denied participation in the common table. (RB 43.13, 15)

In our society, people do not seem to take table manners so seriously. Families do not usually insist on careful table etiquette like they used to. Today the struggle seems to be to find a time when all the members of the family can sit down together to eat. In my family, we were not allowed to leave the table unless excused, nor were we permitted to stand by the table while others were eating. When I worked as a table waiter in the monastery, it used to miff me when those who had already eaten felt free to stand around our "second table" to kibbitz and occasionally reach in and snatch a morsel like some ill-bred oaf. Even more countercultural is Benedict's idea that he can punish people by excluding them from the common table.

Nowadays, the problem is that too many exclude *themselves* from it!

March 19

If she still stands firm, the Rule should be read to her again after four months. And if after considering the matter carefully she promises to keep everything and do everything she is told, then she should be accepted into the community. (RB 58.13-14)

Why is the Rule read three times to the novice? Adalbert de Vogüé notes that Benedict has a fondness for the number three, which appears often in this chapter. But there is a more cogent explanation, also from de Vogüé. He points out that Benedict has in fact amalgamated two separate chapters on monastic formation from the Rule of the Master. Since the Master has the Rule read once to transferring monks, and twice to new lay recruits, Benedict conflates this into three readings. This has nothing much to do with modern monastic formation, but to recognize the background could save us some guilt about ignoring the ancient details. At any rate, Benedict's point is clear enough: the novice should be clearly confronted with the Rule, and not just the letter of it but the whole reality of monastic life. Without knowing that, she cannot make an adult commitment.

March 20

No one should pursue what he judges advantageous to himself, but rather what benefits others. (RB 72.7)

Father Bernard was thirsty. The drive from Devils Lake was long and hot, and the company was not good. In this case, the company was Father Mark, who drove the car and at whose chaplaincy Bernie would stay that night. Mark had a way of setting Bernie's teeth on edge with his narrow-minded views on all subjects and his massive self-righteousness. But it was his car and his house, so Bernie had to go along with it. Actually, Bernie wondered what he was in for that night, since Mark had a reputation for stinginess. When they came into the kitchen, Mark said with an air of genuine magnanimity: "Man, a beer would go good right about now. How about it Bernard?" So Mark rummaged in the fridge and came out with two bottles. Unfortunately, one of them had been placed too close to the freezing unit and was solid ice. "Too bad," said Mark, "yours is frozen!"

March 21

Wherever we are, we are slaves of the same Lord and soldiers of the same King. (RB 61.10)

In chapter 61, Benedict discusses the treatment of visiting nuns. In general, he counsels openness. We should learn all we can from the visitor, and if she expresses a wish to transfer to our community, we should give this serious consideration. Then comes the rationale found in this verse. In this context, it seems to mean that it makes little difference *where* we serve the Lord, as long as we serve him. But Benedict may feel a twinge of guilt about this fairly flimsy argumentation, for a few verses later he insists that such a nun not be accepted without leave of her previous community. The same rationale was used in chapter 2 (v. 20) for a better purpose: all should be treated equal because all serve the same Lord. And so it is plain that

Benedict, like every religious commentator (including me), has his good days and his bad days. And it is also plain that a theological dictum depends heavily on the use to which it is put.

March 22

If one of the priestly order asks to be admitted into the monastery, do not be too quick to say yes. But if he persists in his request, he should know that he will have to observe the full discipline of the Rule. (RB 60.1-2)

Another abbot might be delighted to have priests seeking admission to his monastery, but Benedict is cautious. In this, he is not alone. Earlier founders, such as Pachomius, resisted ordination and did not encourage it for their brothers either. Why? The usual reason given is pride. Priesthood traditionally was glamorous, and priests were fawned over. Some encouraged it and some did not. Benedict warns the priest-novice that his salad days are over. He will be just one of the gang in the cenobium. If he has a true cenobitic vocation, such a warning will come as a relief, not a threat. After all, anyone with eyes can see that adulation has not been good for priests. It has ruined some of them, and that includes monk-priests. But monastic humility has made monk-priests attractive to the greater church. Lately, some monk-priests have been made bishops.

March 23

The blessing of obedience is not only something all the sisters should render to the prioress, but to each other as well. For they know that they will go to God by this route of obedience. (RB 71.1-2)

Even though the Holy Rule is shot through with obedience, it often strikes us as something harsh and intimidating. Here, though, obedience has a kind of fluid quality. It is not only vertically aimed at the superior; it is horizontally aimed in *all* directions as mutual obedience. That should suit our modern sensibility. But it is not so easy. Many nuns find it quite intimidating to remain open to the authority and influence of *all* their sisters. It is much easier to accommodate the wishes of one superior than those of many persons, especially when they seem contradictory. Hard as it is, Benedict does not hesitate to call it a "blessing" *(bonum)*. Remember that in the Prologue he also called it a *labor*. Often you hear it spoken of somewhat sardonically, as if it were something to be put up with. Not here! Here it is the route, the means, by which we go to God.

March 24

The third step of humility is to submit to the superior in all obedience for the love of God. In this, we imitate the Lord, of whom the Apostle says: "He became obedient to the point of death" [Phil 2:8]. (RB 7.34)

Although at the end of the ladder of humility (7.67) Benedict claims that the ladder leads from fear of God to love for God, he adds the love of God to the third step of the ladder. Perhaps he sees that there is a danger of restricting love to a high level of spirituality, a thing sanctioned by John Cassian but not by the New Testament. This short passage makes the important point that, far from being an easy matter, obedience to a superior is experienced by many monks as quite difficult. Although the quote from Philippians 2:8 does not mean that it almost kills people, nevertheless, the comparison of monastic obedience with the death of Christ shows that this is serious business. The implication is that the obedient Christ is quite willing to accompany the monk on the sometimes bloody trial of obedience to an abbot. Without the help of Christ, one can hardly negotiate this aspect of cenobitic life.

March 25

Are you willing to put aside your own will? (RB Prol. 3)

Although many translations have "self-will," that is not exactly right. It would be an easier reading, but not the correct reading. Lest it seem that there is little difference between the two, it should be insisted that in Christian spiritual jargon, "self-will" is always a vice to be rooted out. It refers to the sinful human drive for autonomy and independence from all outside control. On the contrary, everybody has their "own will" and it cannot be set aside in any absolute sense. If we were to press Benedict on this point, he would probably admit that he does not mean that we may ever totally give over our will to the wishes or directives of another human guide. Of course, the reference here is Christ himself, so the point is well taken. One of the principal maxims of most Christian spiritual masters is that we must seek above all things the will of God and conform our own will to it. But it is also imperative to remember that the goal of a healthy Christian, monastic program is transformation of the will, not the eradication thereof.

"Do not return evil for evil" [1 Pet 3:9]. Do no wrong to others,
but suffer patiently the wrongs done to you. "Love your enemies"
[Matt 5:44]. Do not curse those who curse you, but bless them instead.
"Bear persecution on behalf of justice" [Matt 5:10]. (RB 4.29-33)

At this point Benedict sees fit to include in his Rule some of
the hardest injunctions in the entire New Testament, namely,
the ones that forbid the Christian from taking vengeance. It
should not be imagined that monks find these admonitions
any easier than other Christians do. In fact, one sometimes gets
the impression that a certain kind of hatred flourishes more in
monasteries than elsewhere. This is what the ancient Greeks
called *maenis,* a cold, implacable resentment that only manifests itself in the most indirect, "passive-aggressive" forms.

Once an old monk said to a young one: "You know, you
fellows worry me. In the old days we used to shout at each
other and even throw furniture, but we got it out. You smolder
like a bunch of Siamese cats." Of course, the best thing would
be to have no enemies, no resentments. But to be a disciple of
Jesus at least means to absorb mistreatment and hatred without perpetuating the chain of evil by retaliation.

March 27

If one of the deans is found to be puffed up with pride and needs to
be corrected, he should be warned once and again and a third time.
If he refuses to change, he should be expelled from his deanship and
replaced by another who is worthy. (RB 21.5-6)

This kind of warning, coming as it does at the end of a rather
serene and lovely little chapter, may not seem worthy of

comment. Actually, all too many of Benedict's chapters end this way and leave a sour taste in the mouth. Could it be that another hand has gone back through the Rule and tacked on these warnings? Literary criticism indicates this is rather unlikely, but it is possible. Overall, Benedict does not seem to be a pessimistic personality. Yet he is certainly a realist and someone who lived long years among monks. As such, he knows that things can go bad, people included. Sometimes "power corrupts" and has to be rebuked. People may even have to be removed from their jobs. That is the sad task of the superior, and when he or she hasn't got the courage to do it, things can go from bad to worse. Who will "bell the cat"?

March 28

It is the abbot's responsibility to make the decision for a noon meal if there is work in the fields or there is a heat wave. He should arrange things with such moderation that souls might be saved and the brothers can do their work without justifiable murmuring. (RB 41.4-5)

The normal mealtime for Benedict's monks was 3 p.m., when the single meal of the day was taken. Here, though, the abbot is instructed to move the meal forward to noon (a light meal was also taken in the evening) in certain circumstances. The reasons given here are work and heat, although we might wonder about the latter one. At any rate, it is evident that the author wants the abbot to humanize the system and make sure that charity prevails over discipline. What is more, Benedict does not hesitate to tie this kind of minor administrative decision to the ultimate purpose of the monastery: to save the souls of the members. Some scholars think that "souls might be saved" is code language for the principle that spiritual values are to be preferred to material ones. Whether that is so or not, it is clear that Benedict does not want to crush people, nor does he want to drive them to bitter despair.

March 29

If someone is offered something by the superior and turns it down, but then decides later that he wants what he previously refused, he should receive absolutely nothing until he has made fitting amends. (RB 43.19)

On the face of it, this regulation smacks of a kind of paternalism that is no longer fashionable, or even tolerable, in most monasteries. Still, it is not necessary to read it that way. Instead of acting on a mere whim, the superior here may be responding to special conditions that seem to mandate special food and drink for the monks. Benedict speaks of that especially in regard to summer work (39.6; 40.5; 41.4-5) and seems to consider it a regular practice. It is a good example of monastic authority taking good care of people. For the monk to refuse to be taken care of seems to exasperate Benedict—and well it might. For when people will not accept necessary assistance, they invariably end up taking care of themselves. "I want what I want when I want it."

March 30

Now if the newcomer continues knocking and shows that she bears patiently for four or five days the rebuffs offered her and the difficulty of entrance, and if she persists in her request, then let her come in and stay in the guest room for a few days. (RB 58.3-4)

Did Benedict actually treat those who came to his door so roughly? Or was this merely a kind of ritual of reluctance that everyone knew was but a formality? That is exactly what it is in the Rule of the Master (RM 90.2). Some hermits were quite harsh to those who wished join them, for example, Palamon to Pachomius (*Life of Pachomius*, G1 6), warning them that they were undertaking a hard path. Cassian (*Inst.* 4.7) claims that cenobites used to have their postulants live a while in the guest house, but not as guests. They were to help the guest master serve the pilgrims. Surely that apprenticeship would teach them the kind of patience that Benedict demands. One thing is sure: We should not be babying our novices. We should not be persecuting them either, but they need to learn to face the challenge of the ethics of Jesus.

March 31

For their part, the sick should keep in mind that they are being served out of respect for God. Therefore they should not irritate, by their excessive demands, the brothers serving them. (RB 36.4)

One day the phone rang in the abbot's office. It was Brother Paschal calling from the hospital. He was a hemophiliac and the doctors could not stop his bleeding, no matter what they did. "Father Abbot, the doctor wants to operate but I don't want it." "Why not?" "Because I am old and my day is over. Let me die." "You just do what the doctor wants, Brother Paschal." The doctor succeeded in stopping the flow with a special drug. This pleased Brother Paschal, since he presumed it saved the monastery a lot of money. Therefore he was shocked later when he opened his mail and found a bill for $85,000. He rushed to the procurator, who also wondered if a zero had been added by mistake. From there the case went to the abbot, who called the doctor. "Well, did you want us to let him die?" the abbot was asked.

April 1

The sisters should approach for the kiss of peace and for Holy Communion, to intone a psalm or to stand in choir, according to the rank determined by the prioress or by their date of entry. (RB 63.4)

Statio was prominent from the earliest beginnings of cenobitism. For example, Jerome says that the Pachomians lined up in seniority for various liturgical functions (Rule of Pachomius, Pref. 3). Strict hierarchy was practiced in our American monasteries in table seating, choir order and so forth. But this kind of arrangement was at sharp variance with the informal and egalitarian nature of modern western culture. Therefore, it is no surprise that it should evaporate with many other ancient customs once "renewal" was undertaken. Although it should be countercultural, monasticism normally shares some elements of its own time and place. Hierarchy was typical of traditional society; it is no longer typical of ours. Still, it is possible to ask whether this change has influenced us to respect one another more or less? Has it made it easier to love one another?

April 2

If [a visiting nun] is content with the local customs . . . let her stay as long as she likes. If, though, she criticizes some shortcoming calmly and with loving humility, the prioress should consider the matter carefully. Indeed, the Lord may have sent her for that very purpose. (RB 61.2, 4)

Benedict recognizes that local communities may be quite isolated, and that outside criticism can be very helpful. For their part, outsiders should be rather slow to come to conclusions. Experience has shown that first impressions can be very misleading. For example, a community that can seem quite cold and aloof for a casual visitor, may turn out to be very different if one stays around a few weeks. How can we tell if an outsider is worth listening to? Benedict recognizes that these are not easy matters to decide. But he suggests that if such a person is not selfish or egotistical, we can find it easier to listen to them. Of course, we should be open to the truth in whatever form it takes, but when it is proffered "calmly and with loving humility," it is more palatable.

April 3

Just as there is a bad and bitter zeal that separates us from God and leads to hell, there is also a good zeal that separates us from vice and leads to God and eternal life. (RB 72.1-2)

This famous verse is an "antithetical parallel," juxtaposing two similar ideas but so as to emphasize their difference. Obviously, the common denominator here is "zeal," a fairly unusual English word meaning enthusiasm or passion for something. We are more familiar with its derivative "jealous," which is a negative form of zeal. Actually, Benedict speaks in a couple of places of bad zeal (4.66; 64.16 and 65.22) when it implies a power struggle in the community. Surely the religious hatred we see at work today is a form of bad zeal. Given his abhorrence of disorder, we might expect that Benedict would therefore avoid "zeal" altogether. Yet he knows very well that all true religion depends on it in the form of love. As Christians, we believe that God's love for us is the essential energy of our faith; and we are told to love one another with that same love.

April 4

The fourth step of humility is this: when obedience involves hard and unpleasant things, or even unjust injuries of some sort, one embraces them patiently and with no outcry. (RB 7.35)

This is one of the hardest verses of St. Benedict's Rule to translate. That may be because the manuscripts have garbled the word *constantia* (courage) with *conscientia* (no outcry). Another difficulty lies in the content, which seems to be talking about injustice suffered by a monk from monastic authority. The early monastic rules do not usually admit that such things can happen, but they certainly can. Admittedly, it is rarely deliberate, but the monk may well *experience* authority as unjust. What then? Benedict urges the monk to persevere and not give up the struggle. This is a special form of humility, since it is definitely *not* sought as some of the other steps might be. The word "embrace" does not mean one goes looking for such trials. The New Testament calls for perseverance in the face of bloody persecution. Benedict, however, quietly drops the word *martyr* from the text of the Master. Perhaps he does not wish to promote a persecution complex.

April 5

Therefore we must establish a school for the Lord's service. (RB Prol. 45)

There was a sort of scholastic atmosphere among the early monks in the Egyptian Desert. Typically, seekers would live with a "father" or "mother" who would teach them monastic wisdom. This teaching would be characterized by a request for a "word of life" and often it would involve personal imitation of the lifestyle of the "master." This semi-anchoritic model is much in evidence in the Rule of the Master, but not in the Rule of St. Benedict. Of course, it is possible that a given abbot has a body of doctrine, and monks can be termed "disciples," but that is not the usual pattern we find in RB. Benedict's abbot is expected to be a teacher, but he is also considered a "disciple" of the Rule itself (see RB 3.11). It has to be remembered that a community outlasts one person. If the superior is too influential as a monastic teacher, it can be very hard to transfer authority to the next leader. What is more, it is not normal for people to remain in "school" all their lives, but monks should be open to instruction no matter what their seniority.

April 6

Take up the powerful, shining weapons of obedience to fight for the Lord Christ, the true King. (RB Prol. 3)

Perhaps the key point is to recognize that the battle that Benedict is talking about is not against external foes whether the enemies of the Church or the individual soul. Rather, this is an allusion to the warfare within, the struggle of the individual to overcome sin and arrive at spiritual maturity. Of course, the mention of "Christ the true King" could make us think of the cosmic battle between the Kingdom of God and the power of the devil. Surely the individual drama is part of the larger one. But the Lord Christ is also the chief commander in the struggle of the self to attain full stature. Indeed, the Bible and the church fathers often speak of this process as the conformity of the soul to the image and likeness of Christ. The enemy in this battle is anything that retards the self from profiting from this process of transformation. We come to personal realization by putting aside our private agendas to serve the great commander, the Lord Christ.

April 7

Put your hope in God. When you see something good in yourself, credit it to God, not to yourself. As for evil, know that you are always the cause of it and take full responsibility. (RB 4.42-43)

These verses from the chapter, "What are the Tools of Good Works?" are of special interest to philosophical theologians and historians of Christianity. They seem to be an extremely strong expression of the Augustinian teaching that we ourselves can do nothing good; God alone is the source and origin of all good. But when it comes to evil, Augustine insists God has nothing to do with it. This may follow an impeccable theological logic, but it is much harder for human psychology. In an age when so many people suffer from a lack of self-esteem, it is tough to stomach the idea that we can take no credit at all for our good works. What else do we have to fall back on? The first verse is helpful here: "Put your hope in God." After all, the spiritual life is really not a calculus of who accomplishes what and who deserved what. All we need to know is that God loves us and is present to us—even in our struggles.

April 8

They ought to sleep clothed and girded with belts and cords . . . And so the monks will always be ready to rise without delay when the signal is given. (RB 22.5-6)

Since it seems to refer to sleeping customs so different from our own, and since the spiritual message is not so clear, chapter 22 is easy to overlook. But in fact a number of important Benedictine themes come together in this little treatise on the monastic dormitory. One of them is vigilance. Although sleep as such is a kind of abandonment to oblivion, Benedict wants to resist that element. Since the monks must proceed directly to the Office of Vigils from sleep, it is necessary that they be ready to do so. In addition to sleeping clothed, the medieval monks placed their dormitory right off the transept of the church, with a staircase leading from bed to choir. Indeed, some liturgists claim that the Night Office itself is the premiere monastic Office which identifies the special role of monks: while the rest of the world sleeps, we watch for the Lord.

April 9

If any sister, however, is rebuked for the slightest reason by the prioress or any one of her seniors in any way whatsoever, or if she sees that a senior is even faintly perturbed at her or disturbed in any way, she should then and there prostrate on the floor and lie at her feet making satisfaction until the disturbance has been healed by a blessing. (RB 71.6-8)

These are shocking verses. The tone is completely extravagant, and the doctrine radical. To claim that one must always capitulate to one's elders is to preclude all change. How can Benedict forbid all challenge to the authority of seniors? Of course, he can do so in the name of humility. No doubt a given individual can make spiritual progress by putting aside her ego to give in to the senior. But the verse makes much less sense if seen from the standpoint of the senior. If she is to be indulged in all circumstances, how will she ever learn the hard truth about herself? How will she ever overcome her anger? How will she avoid remaining a spiritual infant? Perhaps Benedict should have labeled this chapter: "To be read with special care. Parental guidance needed."

April 10

One who is excommunicated for serious faults from oratory and table should lie prostrate and silent outside the entrance to the oratory at the time when the celebration of the Divine Office is completed. (RB 44.1)

In the early church, those who had committed major sins were not immediately received back into the community; they had to prostrate in sackcloth at the church door week after week. Likewise, the monk who has erred grievously against the community cannot expect quick forgiveness. The gesture of prostration is one of the most dramatic and effective signs imaginable. By it, we place ourselves on the lowest level, acknowledging that everyone else is above us. There is some reason to think that the early monks prostrated between the psalms of the Divine Office to give themselves over to silent prayer. This gesture is rarely seen in the church today except on Good Friday, at priestly ordination and monastic profession. But it still has the power to remind us that we are in utter need of God's mercy and help.

April 11

If some of the craftwork is to be marketed, those who carry out the transaction should not dare to engage in any deception. They should remember Ananias and Sapphira [Acts 5:1-11]. (RB 57.4-6)

Can Benedict really be serious when he compares deception in monastic commerce to the sin of Ananias and Sapphira? After all, they were struck dead by God for merely deceiving the Apostles as to the extent of their donation. As a matter of fact, Benedict thinks monastic fraud is even *worse!* Apparently the reason is because monastic goods are consecrated to Almighty God, who is mocked by sharp dealing. It might seem rather preposterous that such unworldly persons as nuns and monks would descend to crooked business practices. Yet monastic business persons can become quite as caught up in the scramble for the almighty buck as anyone else. Any student of church history knows that the lust for money (avarice) has brought the church of Christ into grave disrepute in many times and places. Of course, someone needs to be concerned about paying the bills. But when the bottom line becomes the be-all and end-all, we are on a very slippery slope.

April 12

Visit the sick [Matt 25:36]. (RB 4.16)

Brother George did not like Father Theodore. He did not hate him, because he knew Christians should not hate each other, but he disliked him so much that Theodore stayed away from him. Even when George was on his deathbed, he did not visit him because he was afraid it would just worsen his condition. But finally George was *in extremis* and the whole brotherhood was taking turns on the deathwatch. Theodore decided it was time to visit because George was probably only semiconscious and beyond caring who it was who sat there. When Theodore came into the hospital room, a postulant named Jeff was sponging the face of George, who was still very conscious. Theodore tried to signal Jeff to pay him no attention and keep his mouth shut, but he did not get through. "Oh look, Brother George, here is Father Theodore! Now you are in good hands!" he crowed. With that, George emitted a loud groan and rang for the nurse.

April 13

In addressing one another, no one is permitted to call another by her simple name. (RB 63.11)

Names are very important in community life. How we address people says a lot about what we think of one another. In the days before Vatican II, novices were warned not to call each other by their nicknames. Benedict says we should not even use "simple names," meaning without a title such as "Brother." But traditional novices soon noticed that the older members of the community did indeed call each other by their simple names, and it did not seem to imply any lack of respect. This is a matter that depends very much on context. If one lives in a highly formal society, simple names could denote lack of respect. But if one lives in an informal one, the use of titles might seem very stiff and cold. A. de Vogüé, citing the *Life of Fulgentius of Ruspe,* says that for all its political chaos, the sixth century was indeed an age of formality. Therefore Benedict was simply echoing his times. But in the present United States, titles generally make people uncomfortable. We ought to address people in the way that they themselves prefer.

April 14

The prioress must be careful never to offer hospitality to a nun from another known monastery, except with the consent of her prioress or letters of recommendation. For it is written: "What you do not want done to yourself, do not do to anyone else" [Tob 4:16]. (RB 61:13-14)

Although we do not know much about them, it is clear that there were several monasteries in Italy in the sixth century. Otherwise, why would Benedict be sensitive to the feelings of other superiors? We might feel that this network was a little too tight. Why not let individuals move freely about? Why hem them in with bureaucratic, proprietary measures such as letters of recommendation? Sometimes it is good for a nun to make a completely new start in another community. Still, the new prioress ought to know at least something of her reasons for leaving the previous monastery. And then there is the matter of "poaching." Strange as it sounds, superiors have been known to captivate members of another monastery to the extent that they leave to join "the Pied Piper." This is hardly a recipe for fruitful intermonastic relations.

April 15

"*Whether All Should Receive Necessities in Equal Measure*"
(RB 34.0—title)

The question asked by the title expects the answer NO. But how can that be, since surely everyone deserves to receive what they need? The salient word is "equal measure," which is in fact the main point of the chapter. Benedict is a nuanced thinker. He is not like certain ideologues who have ruined modern economies by ignoring the differing needs of people. If one practices a strict form of distributive justice, each one gets the same portion. For Benedict, however, each one should receive what she needs: no less and no more. That way, the differences between persons will be respected and no one will go away needy. This does not mean that this system will be without problems, since some people will not be satisfied with getting enough—they want what others have. This is what Eric Auerbach called *mimesis,* envy of others that lies at the root of all violence. This chapter attempts to explain why *unequal* distribution is necessary.

April 16

The fourth step of humility is this: when obedience involves hard and unpleasant things, or even unjust injuries of some sort, one embraces them patiently and with no outcry. (RB 7.35)

Many pious commentators take this verse to mean that the monk is completely passive in the face of injustice if it comes from above. Some even suggest that monastic humility must conform its ideas to the ideas of those in authority, even when convinced that those in authority are wrong. Neither of these conclusions is warranted. For one thing, the words "with no outcry" are by no means certain in the text; they may be a garbled form of "quiet courage"! At any rate, such interpretations show no awareness of the concept of "nonviolent resistance." When one comes into conflict with authority, one is not called to renounce one's views but rather to make them known in a humble way. If this expression results in some kind of overt retaliation by authority, then one accepts it as the price of truth. But one does not renounce one's truth—for anyone.

April 17

In organizing the "school for the Lord's service" we have tried not to create anything harsh or oppressive. (RB Prol. 45)

This ostensibly bland and reasonable comment may look a bit different in the light of some other ancient monastic documents. Cassian, for example, argues that newcomers to the monastery be purposely given artificial hardships to test them. The Rule of the Master also suggests that the one who comes knocking at the door be treated rudely. But his heart is not in it, and he quickly admits them. For his part, Benedict is also somewhat cold to the postulant at the gate (58.1-3), but he shows no enthusiasm for a sustained regimen of penance. In the long course of Christian monasticism, however, some organizers have focused on little else but ascetic penance (Abbot de Rancé) and monks in general have been regarded as penitents. Benedict knows that *life itself* will bring "harsh and oppressive" trials at times (RB 58.7), and he seems unwilling to systematically augment this element. This does not preclude, however, a fairly stern regime for monastic neophytes to harden them for a life of full obedience.

April 18

When you prepare to do some good work, you should beg God with earnest prayer to bring it to completion. (RB Prol. 4)

The whole Prologue urges the recruit to undertake the monastic life, which is the "good work" referred to here. But there is a real danger that an overemphasis on strenuous activity could result in what is traditionally called Pelagianism, the notion that we can attain salvation by sheer willpower and hard work. We cannot; the only One who can ultimately save us is God alone, and that is why any good work should be inaugurated with earnest prayer for divine grace. Read in a certain way, this verse seems to give us the credit for beginning the work and for carrying it out, with God relegated to the final task of completing it. Elsewhere (see 4.42-43), Benedict shows that he knows very well that the entire impulse for the good, beginning, middle and end, comes from God. While it is true that the monastic life demands hard striving, it is totally dependent on grace.

April 19

Fear the Day of Judgment. Have a healthy fear of hell. Long for eternal life with the desire of the Spirit. Keep an eye on death every day. (RB 4.44-47)

All four of these aphorisms from the chapter, "What are the Tools of Good Works?" relate to death. But a closer inspection reveals that three of them have to do with fear, while the third one is much more positive. There is no doubt that people throughout much of the history of Christianity have had a powerful fear of death and the judgment. As for a desire for eternal life, that is usually found only among the saints. Still, every now and then one runs across an "ordinary person" who looks forward to heaven. But in our age of advanced secularism, the typical attitude toward the last things is neither dread nor longing, but indifference. Recently a monk returned from a family visit to Las Vegas and his remark was: "No wonder people no longer long for heaven. They have it here and now." Another monk responded, "That's funny. When I visited Vegas twenty years ago, I experienced it as a foretaste of hell!" It all depends on your point of view.

April 20

Each one should try to arrive at the Work of God before the others—of course with dignity and modesty . . . . They should gently encourage one another to counter the excuses of the sleepyheads. (RB 22.6, 8)

We seem to have here a kind of holy footrace, perhaps something like that of Peter and John on Easter morn (John 20:1-9). As odd as that may seem, holy competition actually shows up several places in the Rule, especially in verse 72.4: "Let them be the first to show honor to one another." Notice, however, that the usual dynamics of competition are inverted, for there is no question of winners and losers. Instead, the swifter make sure the slower are *not* left behind. Likewise, Benedict makes sure that his "race" from the dormitory to the choir is not a dog-eat-dog competition. Those who find it easier to rise and shine are to gently encourage those who do not. When we see the deeply worn stone steps leading down from the dormitory to church at a ruined monastery like Fontenay, it is hard not to think of this lovely little passage from the famous Rule that made it all happen.

April 21

[Monastics] should ask for all they need from the father of the monastery. And they may not have what the abbot does not give or permit. (RB 33.5)

The basic impulse for chapter 33 comes from Cassian (*Inst.* 7), who argues that avarice stains the soul and must be completely expunged. But avarice also has another problem for the cenobite: it cuts him off from monastic authority. Therefore it is a form of disobedience. The issue here is dependence or independence. If I can obtain the necessities of life without asking the abbot or anyone else for them, then I am a free economic agent. At least that is one way of looking at the matter, but not Benedict's way or Cassian's way. Granted, it can be vexing to have to ask for what is needed. Yet it still brings freedom from care, as Cassian puts it. At one time, monastics, especially women, felt they needed to handle their own personal budget. They had good reasons to feel this way, but some of them found out it was just another nail in the coffin of cenobitic solidarity.

April 22

Then, if the abbot commands it, he should be received back to his place in choir, or to the place decided by the abbot. He should not, however, presume to perform a psalm or lesson or anything else unless again the abbot gives the order. (RB 44.5-6)

When a monk has been excommunicated from the Divine Office because of some serious fault, Benedict is in no hurry to reinstate him. Unlike the author of the Rule of the Master, he does not appear to feel the need to rush to a solution of the problem. Rather, he insists on a rather slow, elaborate ritual of reintegration, so much so that the reader may feel uneasy. What could be the point of this? Perhaps it is to insure that the healing would not be superficial. That could prove worse than *no* solution. In addition to its leisurely pace, Benedict's ritual of reconciliation gives a very prominent place to the abbot. In fact, the abbot is named no less than eight times in chapter 44. This means that the healing process is not automatic or impersonal, but one that is carefully monitored by the pastor of the monastery.

April 23

The prioress should provide people with everything they need: that is, cowl, tunic, sandals, shoes, belt, knife, stylus, needle, handkerchief, writing tablets. (RB 55.18)

It seems as if the intent of the author is to provide a basic kit for each sister; beyond that, everything would be held in common. It can come as something of a shock to stay in a monastery of the "primitive observance" where one's bedroom has no cabinets but only three hooks. Where do the monks put all their clothes? Apparently almost all the clothing is kept in common closets. Probably most people would find this excessive, but at least it calls into question our American need to surround ourselves with mountains of private possessions. Monastic rooms are no exception: they burst with chattel. Perhaps this plethora of goods does not violate Benedictine poverty *strictly speaking*, but it does seem to undercut its spirit. A good experiment would be to see how little we can live with. If nothing else, it will simplify the job of those who must clean out our room after we die.

April 24

When he has no material goods to give to someone who asks, he should at least return a friendly word. (RB 31.13)

"Good morning, Brother!" said Father Timothy, as he passed Brother Oscar in the hallway. Tim did not know what else to say to the old man since he refused to discuss with him the only obvious topic of mutual interest, namely, the weather. Oscar was the monastery weatherman. He would give some people a detailed analysis of that subject, but Tim was definitely not one of those people. But this morning he was in an even fouler mood than usual: "Don't say good morning to me!" barked Oscar. "That's all you ever say to me and it means nothing." "Well," said Tim, "maybe we should explore some other topics?" "No," said Oscar, "you and I have nothing in common." "Let's sit down and see if we don't have more in common than you may think," said Tim. So Oscar grudgingly sat down and they ran through the list of possibilities: Renewal in the Church, national politics, the music of Lawrence Welk and so on. In the end, though, it turned out that Oscar was right: they had nothing in common except their humanity and their baptism in Jesus Christ.

April 25

When a senior passes by, a junior should rise and offer her a place to sit; the junior should not presume to sit down until the senior tells her to do so. That will satisfy the biblical command: "They should try to be the first to show respect to the other person" [Rom 12:10]. (RB 63.16-17)

With all due respect to Benedict, this piece of monastic etiquette will not "satisfy the biblical command" of Romans

12:10. In that verse, St. Paul urges Christians to full mutuality. Every one of them, not just the junior, should compete in paying honor and respect to the others. Although Paul often defers to ancient social differentiation, he is here teaching radical Christian equality: In Christ there is no junior or senior. Having said that, it must be admitted that the courtly courtesy recommended in this verse has much to recommend it. In traditional societies, the old were (and are) respected simply for their venerable age. They are deferred to as a mark of love for the *community itself.* Strictly speaking, "senior" and "junior" for Benedict does not denote chronological age. Still, it is hard to keep age out of the picture in this verse.

April 26

If the abbot seeks to have a priest or deacon ordained for himself,
he should choose one of his monks who is fit to exercise the priesthood.
(RB 62.1)

The Latin could just as well read "for them" instead of "for himself," but it is quite possible that Benedict sees this question in different terms than we do today. Nowadays, the abbot is always a priest himself. It does not have to be that way, but it has been that way for twelve hundred years. To judge from the Rule of the Master, however, sixth century abbots were often not priests and they were sometimes in a rather weak position vis-à-vis the local church. If the monastery had to rely on the ministrations of the local clergy, then there was danger that that clergy would eventually dominate the abbot. That seems to be the case with the arrangement in the Rule of St. Augustine. Benedict tries to make sure such things don't happen. Solution? Have one of your men ordained. The corollary is that a monk-priest will be situated firmly *under* the abbot, not above him. The monastery is not a clerical system.

April 27

Whether slave or free, we are all one in Christ and under one Lord,
we bear the same yoke of service [Gal 3:28]. (RB 2.20)

It was one of his first homilies, so Father Victor wanted to do
a good job. Of course, the nuns at the convent would allow for
his inexperience, but he wanted to make a strong point that
every one of them could profit from. Moreover, he was happy
that the daily readings enabled him to dwell on one of his
favorite themes: no favorites in Christ. He had always been
irked by the penchant the local Germans had for rehearsing
their family-trees—as if that could get you into heaven! After
Mass, as was their custom, the nuns invited Victor to breakfast.
Because they had table reading, there was no conversation so
Victor left the table without any feedback. That disappointed
him, since he was sure that he had made a good impression.
Sitting at the same table with him was an ancient nun, Sister
Agatha. She had been present at Mass, but she was almost
completely deaf. "You know," she said in a very loud voice as
soon as Victor departed, "that guy's alright. I knew his grand-
mother."

April 28

But they hope so much in God's reward that they joyfully persevere,
saying: "In all these things we triumph because of him who loved us"
[Rom 8:37]. (RB 7.39)

This verse, from the fourth step of humility, concerns patient
perseverance in the face of injustice, even from lawful authority (the abbot). The biblical warrant from Romans 8 has special

weight because it refers to Christ and, more particularly, to his death and rising for our salvation. In the code language of the New Testament, an apparently generic statement like "who loved us" actually refers to his passion, death and resurrection from the dead. Although step four (RB 7.35-43) presents multiple scriptural warrants to bolster its very hard teaching about humility in the face of persecution, this verse of Romans is the most important one. That is so because it spotlights the ultimate foundation for Christian perseverance, the patient perseverance of Christ in the face of death (and unto death). When we walk the lonely road of humble endurance, we know that he walked it before us and that he is still walking it with us. Like him, "we triumph," though perhaps not in this world.

April 29

Considering the good things he has already given us, we should always obey him so he will never disinherit us as his sons. (RB Prol. 6)

Benedict does not merely teach a "feel good" religion, but one based on the New Testament, even in its harder aspects. In the Gospels, Jesus is always presented as kindly and forgiving, but he tells parables that present punishment and even damnation as a possibility for those who reject God's generosity. This particular verse seems to be an amalgam of the famous Prodigal Son (Luke 15:11-32) and the fierce "Parable of the Talents" (Matt 25:14-30). Benedict realizes that our "sonship" is not of the ontological variety: we are not simply "family" with God. Rather, God has kindly taken us to himself as adopted sons and daughters (RB Prol. 5). But this privileged status must not be taken for granted. If we show we do not deserve it, God will disinherit us. Although the verse seems to present God as rather irascible or even vindictive, it can also serve as an antidote to monastic smugness.

April 30

Maintain strict control over your actions at every moment. Know for sure that God sees you wherever you are. When bad thoughts cross your mind, smash them on the rock of Christ by revealing them to a spiritual elder. (RB 4.48-50)

The connection between the first two verses is clear enough. If God sees everything we do, then it won't do to "let ourselves go" now and then. It must be admitted that these ideas do not ring entirely true to the modern ear. Psychologists warn us that constant control can result in a serious breakdown. Furthermore, the image of God peering down from heaven to catch us at our worst leaves us with a God that we do not necessarily want to know. Is this the God with whom we hope to spend all eternity? But we might consider the alternative: that *no one* knows or cares what we do. The idea of smashing bad thoughts on Christ is repeated from RB Prol. 28. It comes from the world of desert monasticism where the relationship between the guru and the disciple revolved largely around mutual awareness and analysis of the inner state of the disciple. Such a relation demands utter candor in the interest of spiritual healing.

May 1

A candle should be kept burning continually in that room until morning . . . The younger brothers should not have their beds next to one another, but intermixed with the elders. (RB 22.4, 7)

Benedict's chapter 22 on the sleeping arrangements for monks is based on chapter 11 of the Master, but it differs in one important way. Whereas the Master explicitly speaks about the dangers of unchastity, Benedict chooses to downplay this element. Still, it is hard to deny that there is some element of concern here as well, for there are many hints of the same problem. Although homosexuality and pederasty have become prominent topics of discussion in the modern church, Benedict says remarkably little about them. Yet it is hard to believe that the psycho-sexual makeup of the old monks was any different from our own. In the *Life of Pachomius*, the founder tells the brothers plainly that many, many homosexual men have applied for entry, but he has not admitted them because he simply does not have the time to provide them with the special guidance they will need living in a cenobium. It is healthier that these matters be openly discussed rather than swept under the carpet.

May 2

Scripture says: "All things should be common to all and no one should presume to call anything his own" [Acts 4:32]. (RB 33.6)

Although the early Christian community was very inspiring for the first monks, the verse from the Acts of the Apostles does not seem to support chapter 33. In fact, the first Christians did *not* eschew all personal property as the monks seemed to think. A closer reading of the text of Acts shows that this verse is in fact a summary that generalizes from one incident. Apparently, Barnabas did sell a farm in Cyprus and give the proceeds to the community, but the whole community did not pool their resources. As for his monks, though, Benedict expects them to do exactly that. For him, this is not a mere ideal but a concrete demand that admits no "ifs" or "buts." That does not mean that monks have ever found this kind of dispossession easy! In fact, our whole culture runs diametrically against it and we have been systematically trained since birth for possession, not dispossession. It requires a whole new way of thinking.

May 3

If someone makes a mistake when chanting a psalm, response, antiphon or lesson, unless he makes humble satisfaction right then and there before all, he should suffer a more severe punishment. For he has refused to humbly correct the fault he committed through negligence.
(RB 45.1-2)

Those who are ready to bowdlerize the Holy Rule will probably drop this little chapter from the schedule of public reading. It seems so utterly alien to our present ethos. Worse than that, it risks sliding over into the realm of magic, where the precise enactment of words and gestures are deemed necessary to achieve success. What we probably have here is a confusion of categories. Benedict certainly does not regard the Divine Office as magic. Thus he does not think that mistakes fall under the rubric of taboo. The real issue lies in the moral realm where pride and humility are in question. To refuse to acknowledge one's own mistake could be a form of real pride. To let everyone see who it was that sang the wrong note can be a healthy form of humility. When these gestures attract too much attention, however, they seem counterproductive.

May 4

If she wants to completely eradicate the vice of private property,
the prioress should provide people with everything they need . . .
That should remove all pretext of unmet needs. (RB 55.18-19)

There are two sides to the coin of monastic dispossession:
Nuns should claim to own nothing of their own, and they
should be supplied with everything they need. In an acquisi-
tive society like our own, this kind of utopian approach to
property is very hard to maintain. We are urged by Madison
Avenue to achieve material autonomy, and we are uneasy when
we feel too dependent on others for our needs. In chapter 33,
Benedict makes rather shocking demands for dispossession,
but in chapter 55 the emphasis is more on the responsibility of
monastic authority to provide for the needs of its dependents.
Strange to say, older monastics seem to have more difficulty
with this discipline than their younger counterparts. Why?
Perhaps because they have lived through traumatic times such
as the Great Depression when they found they could *not* count
on authority to meet their needs. It is very hard to heal the
scars left by this uncertainty.

May 5

Do not give a false kiss of peace. (RB 4.25)

When you first encountered him, Father John looked to be
about 80 years of age. But on his visits to Sacred Heart Abbey,
Father Edward began to suspect he was a good deal older. One
day John remarked that he had gone to school with Abbot

Claude, and that they had graduated from high school together in 1912. A quick calculation told Ed that this made John at least 95 years old. John informed him that he had taught Latin to high school students until the previous year. "Why did you resign?" asked Ed. "I didn't resign!" hissed John. "They kicked me out!" This intrigued Ed, who thought he was retired simply due to extreme old age. But he suspected there was more to the story than that, so he asked Abbot Herbert about it. "Well," said Herb "I hated to do it, but I really had no choice. For one thing, John was getting into the wine cabinet and showing up in class half-drunk. But even worse was the kissing problem." "The kissing problem?" "Yes, he insisted on kissing all the young ladies on the faculty whenever he passed them in the hallway."

May 6

The prioress should ponder on the discretion of holy Jacob, who said: "If I make my flock walk too far, they will all die in one day" [Gen 33:13]. (RB 64.18)

Out of fear of Esau, Jacob declined to accompany his brother on the grounds that his family and his sheep might not be able to keep up because of weakness. Even though Jacob was notorious for his deviousness, his concern was plausible. People can only do so much. A Benedictine prioress, who is in charge of a "total community," must be exquisitely sensitive to the factor of fatigue in her sisters. Although they are all subject to the high ideals of the Holy Rule and the rest of the monastic tradition, the problem is to stay faithful for the long haul. Monastic life is no weekend workshop. The prioress must have a very accurate, realistic sense of "what the trade will bear." When I came to a certain Trappist abbey to give a retreat, I was surprised to learn from the abbot that they would be rising at a rather late hour (for Trappists). "We can't do everything all at once," said the abbot.

May 7

[If a priest does not keep the Rule], he should be considered a rebel, not a priest. If even after frequent warnings he still refuses to amend, the bishop should be brought in as a witness. But if he still does not improve, and if his deeds have come to public attention, he should be expelled from the monastery. (RB 62.8-10)

Perhaps some people cannot imagine how such things as rebellion can happen in monasteries. But they can, and monastic history is littered with the wreckage of these cases. Benedict is sometimes portrayed as a placid, upbeat character who does not use harsh methods. That does not mean, however, that he is naive. By the time he had written the last chapters of his Rule, he had very likely lived among cenobitic monks for a long time. By then he knew that things can go wrong, sometimes very wrong. Therefore, better to be prepared for the worst than to be shocked into paralysis. Monastic authority must be prepared for the worst case scenario. The alternative is a kind of false charity that is willing to sacrifice the whole community rather than confront a serious problem. This is the worst species of cowardice and neglect of duty.

May 8

We must set up for our ascending acts a ladder such as appeared to Jacob in a dream [Gen 28:12]. (RB 7.6)

The reason why Jacob's ladder is such an attractive image for the monastic authors is that it goes *both* up and down, that is, he sees angels ascending and descending on it. For the author of Genesis, what he saw was a symbol for God, but for Benedict it represents the possibility of human ascent to God. The paradox, however, is that this is only possible by spiritual descent through humility. Although Benedict does not mention it, we should remember that it takes a great deal of physical effort to climb a ladder. When this image is applied to humility, it has the advantage of showing that this is by no means an easy virtue to attain. That is because it directly flies in the face of our "pride," which means self-interest. Still, the ladder has the drawback of implying that we can "do it ourselves," "pull ourselves up by our bootstraps," and so on. But if there is any virtue that is *not* attainable by sheer effort, it is humility. At the deepest level, it is strictly a gift of God.

May 9

The fifth step of humility consists in revealing to one's prioress by humble confession all the evil thoughts that enter the heart, as well as secretly committed evil acts. (RB 7.44)

How can anyone be expected to open her whole inner life to authority? Is this not a formula for deception and subterfuge? It must be understood that the historic source of this teaching was the Eastern desert, where a person would typically seek out a spiritual director for the healing of her soul. Just as one does not conceal things from a doctor if one wants help, so too it was expected that *all* "thoughts" would be examined. We note that Benedict has narrowed the subject matter of such disclosure to *bad* thoughts. Furthermore, he wants disclosure to the official cenobitic superior. But that changes the whole discussion. The Catholic Church now prohibits religious superiors from hearing the confessions of their subjects on the grounds that the seal of confession effectively ties their hands.

May 10

Sometimes in a given case we have arranged things a bit strictly to correct vice or preserve charity. (RB Prol. 46)

Benedict insists that certain situations call for firmness. Without at least the possibility of such discipline, it is hard to see how an ordinary group of people, which is what Benedictine nuns and monks usually are, will be able to maintain a healthy and vigorous moral and spiritual tone. Benedict does not invoke discipline for its own sake, but because vice needs to be corrected and love needs to be preserved. These purposes may be achieved by other means, but if not, then strictness is to be applied. The Benedictine abbot need not apologize for employing discipline in a given case, but it should not be the general approach to all problems, and it certainly should not be heavy-handed or vindictive. That can best be avoided by remembering that the ultimate goal of all Christian discipline is love. It is a serious aberration to focus on discipline itself as the point of monastic life.

May 11

We should obey him so he will never disinherit us as his daughters.
Much less will he, like a fearsome lord enraged at our offenses, give us
over to everlasting punishment as wicked servants who did not wish to
follow him to glory. (RB Prol. 6-7)

The image of an angry master beating his slaves may well seem repulsive. Applied to God, it seems downright ill-conceived. Still, the Gospels place several comparable parables on the lips of Jesus. Putting aside our cultural difficulties with this material, we are still left with an abiding truth: we will be judged by the way we live. Or, to shift the emphasis from the external to the internal, it is quite possible for us to squander God's grace and our own potential for development as sons and daughters of God. Copying the Rule of the Master, Benedict sees no reason to shield us from this possibility. To undertake the monastic life is by no means a way of avoiding the high-stakes drama of the spiritual life.

May 12

Close your mouth on evil and perverse talk. Do not indulge in
long-winded conversations. Do not engage in empty babbling and
joking. Do not give yourself over to prolonged or explosive laughter.
(RB 4.51-54)

Although the Rule of the Master seems to prohibit all conversation by monks, and RB 6 runs in the same direction, there are many hints in the Rule of Benedict that the monks did in fact talk to one another. But like all things, talk can be abused.

The two verses concerning laughter tend to trouble modern readers, and it is important that they be accurately translated. Not *all* laughter is excluded, but *the destructive kind* is. Lately some people, usually academics, have promoted the idea that jokes are appropriate in all situations. Such persons are often marked by a lack of humor. In fact, the laughter of a person can tell us much about his inner state. Sometimes it is simply the bubbling up of joy, and makes everyone around feel better. But the braying of some betrays no mirth at all, just a need to make noise. Obviously such raucous laughter is a severe disruption of the healthy silence of a monastery.

May 13

If a brother is found to be defiant or disobedient or arrogant or a murmurer, or if he opposes the Holy Rule in any way or disdains the commands of his seniors, he should be warned once and again by his seniors according to our Lord's command. (RB 23.1)

This verse, which leads off a whole succession of chapters on community sanctions, is meant to set the tone for the rest. Someone who expects to find a list of faults and their corresponding punishments, such as we see in the Irish penitentials, will be surprised to find none. Instead, Benedict is concerned with attitudes, and in fact one unacceptable attitude: bad will. The descriptive words used for what will not be tolerated are evocative: defiant, disobedient, arrogant, murmurer, disdainer. All of these negative traits have in common that they are public defiance. This is a very different matter from covert or discreet opposition. There is also such a thing as *loyal opposition*, which is different. In fact, such opposition can strengthen authority by making sure that it does not become careless or flabby, ceasing to give a good account of its decisions.

May 14

A sister who is full of the fear of God should be assigned to the guest house. (RB 53.21)

As a job description for the guest director, we might find this verse less than helpful. Surely there is more to guest care than this? Certainly the guest director should know how to relate to people. And she must be able to manage what often amounts to a fairly complex operation. Indeed, Benedict indicates that he wants a well-managed system that does not depend on mere adrenalin but careful planning and execution. When the guest arrives, she should find the beds made. But the key quality needed in Benedictine guest care is simply *the fear of God.* Why? Because faith in the divine presence is the basic motivation of our hospitality. And this faith is by no means easy, for the guests often show no outward traces of such presence. Finally, it is crucial that we do not contrast fear of God and God's love. The guest director is the only member of the community that many guests ever meet. All the more reason why she must be an effective witness to God's love.

May 15

If someone is working in the kitchen, the cellar, in serving, in the bakery, the garden or at any craft or any other place—and if he commits some mistake, or breaks or loses something, or errs in any other way in any place, and if he does not come immediately before the abbot and community to confess his fault spontaneously and make satisfaction, when it is found out through someone else, he shall undergo a more severe penalty. (RB 46.1-4)

With its relentless repetition of items, and its rather fanatical tone, this passages falls into the category now called "rant." As such, it often calls forth special pleading on the part of commentators who are intent on preserving Benedict's reputation for equanimity. For myself, I find it comforting to know that even our monastic father had some faults and hang-ups of his own. He had traits that needed, more than anything else, forgiveness. To take him at face value in a verse like this is to risk lapsing into the very religiosity that Jesus warns against. As grownup sons and daughters of Benedict, we ought to recognize when our Holy Father is "out of control" and "talking through his hat." At those times we have a duty to ignore him.

May 16

Those sent on a journey should receive a pair of pants, which they should wash and put back upon their return. The cowls and tunics for traveling should be somewhat better than what they usually wear. (RB 55.13-14)

As a matter of practicality, the early monks probably wore pants on journeys because they rode on horseback. Furthermore, it seems natural to wear better clothes abroad than at home. However, this still leaves open the question of whether monks should wear the same monastic clothing both inside and outside the monastery. In a country like the U.S.A., with its strong tradition of separation of church and state, it has been typical for monks to not wear their habit outside the monastery. This did not apply to Benedictine women. But in most other countries, monks dress like monks in public. Certainly the ancient monastic legislators expected that they would do so. But they also expected that their garb would not be too distinctive. Since the garb of Benedictine men is totally unlike that of their lay contemporaries, this principle has been ignored. There is also something a bit odd about dressing so differently in public and private.

May 17

[The abbot] should choose someone with the advice of God-fearing brothers and make him his prior. (RB 65.15)

Nobody saw it coming. True, the abbot's pre-Lenten conference sometimes included appointments of new officials. In fact, all the officials were expected to resign as an act of humility. But that was just a formality and nobody took it seriously. Imagine their surprise, then, when the abbot suddenly announced that he was naming Father Nicholas as the new prior starting immediately. Of course, no one denied that such an appointment was the abbot's right, or that Nicholas was someone who could work with the abbot. In fact, he had been the loyal servant of every abbot going back several decades. But that did not make him any more popular. Indeed, he was the most unpopular monk in the whole monastery, perhaps in the history of the monastery. So everybody was seething with indignation in the procession out of church. But old Father Alberic brought immediate release and comic relief when he solemnly intoned in his best Shakespearean declamatory voice: "Before this day, no evil hath fallen on our tribe!"

May 18

Since he is merciful, he may spare us now and hope we change for the better. But eventually he will say: "You did these things, and I was silent" [Ps 49(50):21]. (RB 7.30)

By and large, people today do not like to be bullied or threatened in regard to religion. Indeed, it would not be far off the mark to say that an important thrust of Vatican II was to eliminate the atmosphere of fear from Catholicism. Yet it must be added that over the long sweep of church history, many people have found the "fear of the Lord" energizing, not paralyzing. More specifically, many great saints entered the monastery precisely to do penance for their sins. As such, they were responding to a verse like this one which urges us to change while there is still time. Note that the text is not entirely threatening since it takes as its basis the mercy, not the anger, of God. But the biblical quote shows well enough that the patience of God is not without limit. At least we have to admit that we will not live forever and we do not know how soon we shall be judged.

May 19

The sisters should keep to their monastic rank as established by date of entry, merit of life or the prioress' arrangement. The prioress should not upset the flock entrusted to her, nor should she arrange anything unjustly, as if she had absolute power. (RB 63.1-2)

The question of rank is perhaps not too important to the contemporary person, but it was so crucial for Benedict that he devoted a rather long chapter to it. The main idea is this: sisters are ranked by their date of entry. That basic arrangement may be slightly adjusted due to merit or the discernment of the superior. But the fundamental order of the monastery is by date of entry. Such a system may seem arbitrary, and indeed it is. But that is its beauty, for it cuts through all of our artificial human distinctions of class, race, chronological age and so forth. And even though this same hierarchy can seem rather rigid by our fluid modern standards, it has the advantage of providing each member with a "niche" where she belongs. Her place in choir, at table, in *statio,* is hers and no one else's. Such stability is a basis for peace.

May 20

And so all the members will be at peace. (RB 34.5)

Although this is not a quotation, it is very closely related to 1 Corinthians 12:12, 26. The image there is of a living human body where all the members are interconnected. They are not identical, but they are all indispensable. So if one is hurting, the rest will feel the effects. Therefore, no member can be neglected without it affecting the whole body. When all are properly cared for, when their needs are met, then they will be "at peace." Since this dictum occurs in chapter 34 of the Rule, it is primarily connected to material well-being. According to Benedict, when the members' varying needs are being met, there should be peace in the community. But this is earth, not heaven, and sin and confusion often disrupt such peace. In a system such as Benedict's monastery, where the ideal is not absolute equality (distributive justice), perhaps the most typical danger is envy. Rather than satisfaction that my own needs have been met, I compare myself with another who needs and receives more. It is a recipe for unhappiness. To quote Pope Paul VI, "If you want peace, work for justice."

May 21

"Confess to the Lord, for he is good. His mercy lasts forever"
[Ps 105(106):1]. (RB 7.46)

In his fifth step of humility, Benedict uses this verse, among several others, to provide a biblical basis for the practice of the complete disclosure of conscience to the abbot. Like many quoted psalm verses, this one originally meant something quite different. The verb "confess," which connotes sins to Catholics, does not mean that to the psalmist. In the present psalm verse, "confession" is simply an avowal that God is good and his mercy lasts forever. Furthermore, one makes this confession to the Lord, not to a religious superior. Still, the Old Testament very often urges the Jew to give personal testimony in the presence of a third party. Likewise, modern spiritual directors encourage their clients to disclose their *whole* inner life rather than just the bad parts. Indeed, the director should help the disciple discern which parts *are* good or bad. Any really honest disclosure of one's inner life is not easy. It does require a special kind of humility, but "sunshine is the best disinfectant."

May 22

When you experience [a bit of discipline], do not immediately become
afraid and flee the path of salvation which must be narrow at the
beginning. (RB Prol. 48)

The "path of salvation" is based on Matthew 7:15, which presents the Christian "way" as essentially a *narrow* path. The corollary is that any path that seems broad and easy is delusive, for it leads to destruction. This is a philosophical and religious principle that is found in all advanced cultures, including the Greco-Roman and the Jewish. It is not wrong, since it is a well-known fact that authentic human growth never takes place without suffering and struggle. Benedict certainly knows this very well, which is shown by the fact that he draws fairly heavily on the radically demanding Sermon on the Mount. Moreover, of its very nature, monasticism seems inextricably bound up with painful conversion. And it could happen that a newcomer to the monastery, who has accepted all this in theory, finds it shocking in practice. When one is asked to make drastic changes in her life, then romanticism could give way to terror. But it is a mistake to flee at once since this hard regimen is only a means to arrive at love.

May 23

Therefore, let us arise at long last, for the Scripture stirs us with the words: "It is high time we rose from sleep" [Rom 13:11]. (RB Prol. 8)

Benedict has added the connecting word "therefore" to this verse to make it segue from the preceding one about bad servants who deserve punishment. The Master accomplished the same thing by using the words "us lazy-bones," which gives the whole verse more color. But the imagery is still very strong: a long, long sleep which must come to an end! Actually the Master and Benedict have introduced an adverb into the text of St. Paul that makes his point even more emphatic: "at long last." Since Paul is addressing Christians who have long "slumbered" in the limbo of paganism, he would have had every reason to use such language. But apparently the monastic founders felt that even monastic aspirants were virtually escaping a world of sloth and sin. To them, the monastic life was like a second baptismal opportunity to find saving grace. So there is not a moment to waste; one must be up and about!

May 24

Listen intently to holy reading, prostrate often in prayer. Confess your past sins in daily prayer to God with tears and groaning. (RB 4.55-57)

Although the first two verses may well look like a random pair, they probably are not. Nor is their order. The relationship between holy reading *(lectio divina)* and prayer in the mind of the early monks was quite precise. To them, the latter came as a result of the former. In other words, the word of Scripture, which was the normal content of *lectio,* is what drives us to prayer. To put it another way, before we have read Scripture, we do not know what to pray for. Before we talk to God, it is crucial that we listen to what God has to say to us. The translation "prostrate" *(incumbere)* in prayer could also be "give oneself over" to prayer. But we know that complete prostration was in fact a classic posture for prayer. Emphasis on such bodily gestures is now more typical of Greek monasticism than in the West. "Tears and groaning" are frowned upon in our society, but for the old monks they were the normal accompaniment of healthy prayer.

May 25

If he does not reform, let him be publicly rebuked in the presence of all. If he still does not improve, and if he understands the penalty, he should be excommunicated. But if he is insensitive to that, let him undergo physical punishment. (RB 23.3-5)

Since Benedict has a reputation for gentleness and moderation, people are sometimes surprised to learn that he has in fact devoted twelve chapters to punishments (RB 23–30; 43–46). Yet he really does take a moderate approach to the question by means of his step-by-step process of confrontation. As in Matthew 18:15ff., which he has clearly used as a model (through the Rule of the Master), he begins with a small delegation to the culprit. If this is rejected, there is a public rebuke. But if even that does not have the desired effect, then there follows excommunication and even physical beating. Although this might not meet modern standards of human rights, it cannot exactly be called inhuman. Sometimes Benedict himself does not conform to his own "penal code," resorting immediately to rough methods (see RB 2.28); but generally he maintains a compassionate and therapeutic attitude toward wayward monks (see especially RB 27).

May 26

It is written: "Distribution was made to each one according to need"
[Acts 4:35]. We are not talking here about favoritism—God forbid!—
but sympathy for weakness [Acts 4:23]. (RB 34.1-2)

The Acts of the Apostles chapters 2 and 4 were favorite texts for the early monks since they enunciated ideals of community in Christ that were the basis of cenobitism. Benedict does not quote these passages very often, but he does so in regard to the arrangement for the necessities of life. In chapter 33 he uses the passage "No one may presume to call anything his own" to bolster monastic dispossession. In chapter 34 he uses Acts 4:35 to guide the community in its philosophy of caring for the material needs of the members. Unlike some of the earlier monastic rules (Pachomius in at least one text), Benedict does not demand that everyone receive the same common issue. Each should get what he needs. Of course, someone will have to judge those needs, and that will have to be the abbot in consultation with the individual. Admittedly this leaves a wide berth for favoritism, but Benedict wants none of that. For him, sympathy, not prejudice, must be the criterion for just distribution in the monastic community.

May 27

If it is a question of a hidden problem of conscience, he should only reveal it to the abbot or one of the spiritual seniors. For they know how to cure their own wounds and those of others, without divulging them in public. (RB 46.5-6)

The context of these verses is Benedict's system of public excommunication for monastic faults. But if they are private, secret faults with no direct impact on the community, he handles them differently. Such problems should be taken up with a good director or confessor, where they can be dealt with in a pastoral fashion. No doubt Benedict is here in continuity with the spiritual direction of the Desert Fathers of the East. Such counseling laid great emphasis on radical honesty in the interest of deep healing for the client. Sayings from the desert stress that a physician can only help me if I make a complete revelation to him of my symptoms. But the other side of this coin is the discretion demanded of such a healer. Although Benedict proposes the abbot as the logical director, modern canon law forbids him to hear the confession of his monks. But Benedict also calls on other monks as spiritual directors to the community.

May 28

Only (when you follow the Holy Rule) will you attain, with God's protection, to the higher peaks of doctrine and virtue that we have pointed out. Amen. (RB 73.9)

What is the relation of monastic practices (following the Holy Rule) to contemplation (the "higher peaks of doctrine and virtue")? Certainly there is no intrinsic connection, for all kinds of non-monks attain to a high level of spiritual maturity without following the Holy Rule. What is more, in the spiritual life practices as such have to be seen as a mere means to the end of union with God. Still, it has to be insisted that monasticism is very much a set of practices—and not a set of ideas! There is something inherently *concrete* about monasticism; it must be *done*, not merely talked about. Furthermore, even though the monastic practices have symbolic value, it is almost impossible to disentangle the "letter" from the "spirit." We can also note that in many cases, the practice must come before the understanding. That is, before one has *practiced* something like silence, one does not know what it is. Only when we have done it can we know what it means.

May 29

The prior must respectfully do what he is told by his abbot, without acting against the abbot's will and arrangements. (RB 65.16)

Since the previous prior had been deeply unpopular, when he was newly elected, Abbot Samuel wanted to make sure the community would have maximum input in the choice of a new prior. So he held a vote and had the tally counted in public by three monks. Then at a chapter meeting, the Abbot dramatically announced that Father Donald had been elected by a big majority. There was ecstatic applause, but Donald was having none of it. He was a cautious, reticent Old Testament scholar who knew how to bring out the right quotation at the right time. "We can't do this," he said. "It would violate the biblical text." "And which text is that?" asked Abbot Samuel. Donald said, "Thou shalt not yoke the ox and the ass" (see Deut 22:10). At which there was uproarious laughter, but the Abbot wasn't quite done. "And which one am I?"

May 30

If the angels assigned to us report our deeds to the Lord daily, day and night, then, sisters, we must always make sure, as the psalmist says, that God never sees us "falling" into evil and becoming "useless people" [Ps 13(14):3]. (RB 7.29)

In recent times angels have been all the rage. The religious gift shops are rife with the winged creatures. They are embossed on drinking glasses, T-shirts and other commercial items. All in all, we seem to find angels pretty comfortable. In this, we are not wrong, for the Bible usually presents angels as the protectors of humanity. They reveal God's will to us, protect those in danger and often assure us: "Fear not!" (for example, Luke 1:30). But some of the angels in the Bible are menacing, and not so comfortable. Certainly the divine "spies" featured in this text will not be too attractive to many readers. We should be aware, too, that angels are often a symbol for the presence of God himself. In this text they are carrying out the will of God, which is to know all that is going on. RB 7 insists over and over that God is constantly mindful of us. We should return God the favor.

May 31

The juniors should honor their seniors, while the seniors should love the juniors. In addressing one another, no one is permitted to call another by her simple name. The seniors should call their juniors "sister," but the juniors should call their seniors nonna, which means spiritual mother. (RB 63.10-11, 15)

These verses seem to regulate the interface between old and young nuns, but chapter 63 teaches that a "senior" is anyone who arrives at the monastery door before her "junior." Even though there is a good deal of equality in Benedict's monastery, it is not absolute. And so he does not simply say that they should "love one another." Instead, he employs two different terms, "honor" and "love" for these relations. Yet a moment's reflection suggests that Benedict would probably be willing to interchange the terms, for juniors also need honor and seniors certainly need love! In discussing the names they are to use for one another, one wonders if the system does not come apart. Surely the term *nonna* would hardly be appropriate for a young nun, even though she arrived at the monastery door before her companion. The matter of chronological age must figure in here *somewhere*.

June 1

As often as important questions have to be dealt with in the monastery, the abbot should convene the whole community and tell them what is involved. (RB 3.1)

While the Rule of the Master merely tacks the matter of community deliberation to the end of his chapter on the abbot,

Benedict develops it into a separate chapter. This shows how important it is for him. In regard to the subject matter of these "chapter meetings," the Master limits it to the administration of the physical property of the monastery. Benedict, however, imposes no such restriction. If there are important spiritual issues at stake, the community is still convened. The word "important" could also be applied to the whole process, for such discussions are crucial for the well-being of a community. Notice that only the abbot can convene the community in this fashion. It is said that some groups have spent endless hours arguing about what kind of doorknobs to install. Benedict does not believe in wasting the time of the whole group in such a fashion. But on the other hand, the abbot should never neglect to get community input just because he thinks he can expedite things without it.

June 2

The sixth step of humility occurs when a monk is content with low and dishonorable treatment. Regarding all that is commanded him, he considers himself a bad and worthless worker. (RB 7.49)

Although it is not perfectly clear, it seems that the context of step six is work. Now, every monk has to work, and in every culture some work is more prestigious than other work. Once a visiting monk was being driven in the early morning to the airport by another monk, whom he asked: "What do you do around here?" "Nothing" was the answer. "Nothing?" "Well, unless you consider driving people to the airport as something," came the reply. Obviously, such work was considered "low and dishonorable" by the monk, and he had hardly come to terms with it. To judge from the tone of his voice, he despised it and he probably despised himself along with it.

The only antidote to this kind of alienation is to put aside all false notions of what is worth doing: anything that benefits others is worth doing.

June 3

But as we make progress in the monastic life and in faith, our hearts will swell with the unspeakable sweetness of love. (RB Prol. 49)

This is one of Benedict's most significant changes in the text of the Rule of the Master. For the latter, monastic spiritual life is essentially static and penitential. All we can hope for in this world is suffering and a share in the Cross of Christ. Only at death will we move on to a higher, happier plane, namely, the bliss of heaven. Apparently, Benedict found this doctrine an unacceptable way to end the Prologue. And so he inserted a very different point of view: the beginnings of monastic life will probably be hard and even at times grim. But if we are faithful to the "system," not excluding serious personal transformation, we can expect to experience "the unspeakable sweetness of love" already in this life. Put in other terms, Benedict does not see monastic life as simply a forced march of ascetic struggle. For him, the system, if it is lived wholeheartedly, should produce joyful, loving people. Seen this way, Benedict teaches a dynamic spirituality that should be attractive to those who are interested in personal growth in the Spirit.

June 4

Let us open our eyes to God's light. (RB Prol. 9)

Everyone knows the difference between rising in the dark days of winter and doing so in the bright light of summer. For Benedict, the latter seems to be the image but he is not talking about mere sunlight. No, the light that is already shining is "God's light." Now the word he uses for God is *deificum*, which is intriguing to say the least. It is a word with multiple possibilities. At its blandest, it can simply mean "divine." That is the translation given here. But it can also mean "God-making" or "divinizing." If that is the correct meaning, then it would mean that even before we are aware of what is happening, God is busy saving us—or more precisely, making us godly. That is not normal language for Western Christians, who may find it pretentious, but in the Eastern Church, *theosis* or deification is the usual description of what happens in the spiritual life. Even while we are asleep, God may be divinizing us!

June 5

"Do not carry out your physical drives" [Gal 5:16], hate self-will. Obey the orders of the abbot in all things, even if he—God forbid!— acts otherwise. Remember the Lord's command: "Do what they say, not what they do" [Matt 23:3]. (RB 4.59-61)

Although physical drives and self-will are not the same thing, neither are they entirely separate. In an important sense, every living organism must look to its own continuance. This is entirely legitimate, but with human beings it often gets out of hand and becomes crass egotism. I was shocked to find that

I had translated the verse to read "Hate your own will"! (*BR* p. 81). Such hatred, if it is even possible, would be a profound pathology. As such it has nothing to do with Christianity, and any spirituality that promotes it is "part of the problem," not the answer. In general, people joining monasteries in our times seem to suffer from a *lack* of ego-strength (will) and not an excess. Nothing important, and certainly nothing hard, can be accomplished without a strong will. Of course, this sometimes leads to a test of wills with authority, a thing of which Benedict wants no part.

June 6

The degree of excommunication and discipline should correspond to the seriousness of the fault. The judgment of the gravity of faults depends on the abbot. (RB 24.1)

There is a significant difference between ecclesiastical excommunication and the monastic variety. The church sometimes bars persons from Holy Communion, thereby ritually excluding them from the body of Christ. The monks, however, excommunicate by barring members from table or choir (or both). This is essentially an in-house operation, seldom involving expulsion and not touching on the sacraments of the church. Admittedly, this process is very rare in modern times, but it should not be imagined that discipline is no longer necessary in community life. Still, modern persons seem to need different treatment. Very often the problem with modern monks is that they excommunicate *themselves*. How does one convey to such persons that it is lethal for a cenobite to be cut off from the community? Benedict leaves excommunication entirely in the hands of the abbot. While we might worry about arbitrary authority, it is far worse to fall into the hands of a committee!

June 7

The one who needs little should thank God and not be sad. But whoever needs more should feel humble at her weakness, and not gloat over the mercy received. (RB 34.3-4)

Benedict gives these verses as an explanation of his principle that "Distribution be made according to need" (Acts 4:35). He is well aware that this philosophy will not come easy to many persons, depending on their character and upbringing. Basing himself on the Rule of St. Augustine, Benedict seems to be legislating for a community in which tough peasants live cheek by jowl with rich aristocrats. Since the peasant is hardened by life to need very little, she should not envy the treatment afforded the rich. Because these latter come from a soft background, they may need more amenities than the others. When they receive preferential treatment, they should not think it is because of their own worthiness. It is because of their weakness. In claiming that the person who needs more is "weak," Benedict is not disparaging that person, but he is certainly running counter to modern consumerist attitudes. In our society, the person who needs and consumes more is considered the best citizen. Asceticism is countercultural; it slows the economy.

June 8

It is the abbot's responsibility to signal the time for the Work of God, both during the day and the night. He should either give the signal himself or entrust the work to a careful brother. That way, everything will be done at the right time. (RB 47.1)

We might be scratching our heads over this passage, for it seems to encourage micromanagement on the part of the abbot. Like many other items in this ancient Rule, however, we can usually detect a kernel of truth and relevance that would be lost if we gave up on the verse. In this case, it is fairly obvious that the Divine Office is important to Benedict, so important that abbot himself must take responsibility for seeing that it is properly done. But it is hard to understand the importance of this passage without some awareness of the ancient problem of telling time at night. Before the invention of the modern clock, it was very difficult to know exactly what time it was once the sun went down. Someone had to stay awake to watch an hourglass or some such thing. It did not have to be the abbot, but he had to make sure it was done.

June 9

The superior, because she is believed to take the place of Christ, should be called abbess or prioress. This is not because of her pretensions, but in order to show honor for Christ. (RB 63.13)

Since very few female Benedictine superiors in the U.S.A. are abbesses, that title is rarely used. But "prioress" does not seem to have caught on either, at least as a form of address. Most nuns address their superior as "sister" or "mother." In fact, the Rule itself instructs the monks to call the superior "lord and abbot," but that seems out of the question in our democratic society. No abbot asks for that! And yet, every superior does want to be addressed in a respectful way. If she or he is asked to represent Christ in the community, then it is only right and just that this Christ-function be somehow acknowledged in everyday speech. No matter what the Rule says, most Benedictines address each other by their simple names. Yet when they have elected a superior, they instinctively switch to something more formal. In a few societies (Australia, for example), nicknames are so prevalent that even superiors retain them. They are obviously signs of affection.

June 10

In the choosing of a prioress, the proper method is always to appoint the one that the community elects by consensus in the fear of God. Or a part of the community, however small, may make the choice if they are of sounder judgment. (RB 64.1)

It seems so very simple. Just have an election and may the best woman win! But true elections are rare in the Catholic Church, and for most of their history the Benedictines were unable to use this method. Usually, this was because the monastery was controlled by outside powers who installed whom they wished. Nowadays, we are back to true elections and they seem to work very well. Yet Benedict himself seems unsure about it. When he suggests that a small group may be better equipped to make the choice, he may be speaking out of hard experience. Yet he does not tell us how to choose that wiser group. And he does not tell us either how to mollify those who have been disenfranchised. For centuries the Benedictine lay brothers did not have a vote, but they do now and they use it with relish.

June 11

If you are eager to reach the heavenly homeland, with Christ's help carry out this modest Rule for beginners that we have sketched. (RB 73.8)

In this, the penultimate sentence of the Rule, Benedict makes sure that he emphasizes two elements: Jesus Christ and heaven. This should serve as a reminder to us that, whatever else it might seem to be, the monastic life is meant to lead us to heaven. And since we are Christian monks, that journey must take place with Christ and in Christ. Certainly we must do our part, and that means carrying out "this modest Rule for beginners." But we recognize that this is merely the means to the end. The end is heaven, where monasticism will be superfluous. As for Christ, though, he is not merely a means to an end, even to heaven. He is both the way and the end itself. To call heaven the "heavenly fatherland" does not mean that Jesus is somehow left behind. Since "I and the Father are one," we can expect to be one with them in heaven. But none of this eschatological emphasis should distract us from this present life where we already have Christ as our companion.

June 12

Love chastity. (RB 4.64)

As a professor of moral theology, one of Father Boniface's goals was to knock some of the naivete and self-righteousness out of the young monks who were his students. When he was feeling particularly mischievous, he would gaze at them and intone lugubriously: "*Spes ecclesiae* (the hope of the Church).

115

Well, I'm glad *she* has some hope!" On some occasions, Boniface tried to undermine a rigid idea of sin, claiming that the only mortal sin could be committed by one moral theologian murdering another moral theologian in cold blood at high noon in front of St. Peter's. Other times he took the opposite side of things. One day he was carefully explaining the church's doctrine of plenary indulgences. Instead of emphasizing how easy it is to gain one of these dispensations, Boniface was at pains to show that it is almost impossible. Thus, it is not enough that a person merely confess his sins and then say certain prayers. In addition, one must put aside all *attachment* to sin whatsoever. "Well, I guess that leaves me out!" said Boniface sadly.

June 13

The brothers should serve one another. Therefore, no one should be excused from kitchen duty except for ill-health or involvement with an essential task. (RB 35.1-2)

Benedict starts chapter 35 with a programmatic statement that could be taken as the motto for all cenobitic monasteries, indeed, all Christian communities. He then moves to a specific example of this service, namely, cooking and table waiting. Rather than just one example among many, he wants to elevate this particular activity to a special place by insisting that no one should be excused from it. In most modern monasteries, the abbot is excused from kitchen duty on the grounds that his very office makes that impractical. Notice that it is not because of "honor." For Benedict, there is no dishonor in cooking or waiting tables. Yet, to show that this work is of symbolic relevance, the abbot (and perhaps other officials) still wait on table for special occasions. Probably in light of the Last Supper and the washing of the feet (John 13), table service seems to have an abiding importance for Christians. It is endangered by the modern practice of cafeteria service, and especially by the culture of "gulp and run."

June 14

Therefore the days of this life are given to us as a truce for the correction of our faults. (RB Prol. 36)

The symbolism is military, which relates to similar images in Prologue 3 and chapter 1 (vv. 4-5). That style of thought should not be pushed too hard, but certainly Benedict does see the monastic life as a hard struggle. The reference here is to a truce, a breathing space in which we can regroup our forces. Yet that is not exactly right either, since the truce here is mainly to spare us from divine judgment. Indeed, this verse seems to describe life itself as a deferment of punishment for us! That may be harsher than Benedict's actual thought, but there is no doubt that he sees one of the purposes of the spiritual life to be the "correction of our faults." It should be remembered that Benedict is copying here from the Rule of the Master, for whom penance seems to be the *main* purpose of monastic life. Benedict does not go that far, as is evident from verse 49 of the Prologue. Still, the concept of each day as a new chance for conversion is surely an energizing idea.

June 15

[Love] will enable us to race along the way of God's commandments.
(RB Prol. 49)

After admitting that the discipline of the monastic life can be
hard at first, Benedict assures us that its normal result will be a
life of enthusiasm and love. And this love will in turn fuel our
course along the way of obedience to God. The Prologue mentions "running" three times before this, but in those instances,
it is a flight from sin and damnation; here it is a flight toward
God. Some translators render *curritur* simply as "run," and
that is its usual meaning. But in the present verse the context of
holy intoxication seems to call for something stronger. Anybody who has participated in track and field knows that racing
is in quite a different category from mere running; it is closer to
flying than walking. Further, racing is only possible for someone who has transcended the boring routines of conditioning
and arrived at maximum physical fitness. We do not usually
associate this kind of élan with obedience to the commandments, but the Bible does not make a sharp distinction between
obedience and love.

June 16

Let us listen with attentive ears to the warning of the divine voice,
which daily cries out to us: "If you hear his voice today, do not harden
your hearts" [Ps 94(95):8]. (RB Prol. 9-10)

Could it be that the transfiguration of Jesus is the background for this verse? If so, then the sleeping disciples, as well

as we, are addressed by the divine voice. To be sure, God says something else in the Gospel: "This is my beloved Son. Listen to him!" (Mark 9:7; NAB). No matter what he says, it is an astounding thing to be addressed by God at any time or any place. Astonishing enough to silence the garrulous Peter, as he nattered on about setting up three tents. In truth, the word "attentive" *(attonitus)* could be given a more dynamic translation like "thunderstruck." But monks also recognize that there is an element of familiarity here that can be a real hazard, for every monastic Vigil service begins with Psalm 94(95):8: "If you hear his voice today." Since we hear this every morning, we may well grow immune to it, which is equivalent to "hardening our hearts." In fact, one of the hardest tasks of the spiritual life is to remain attentive to the voice of God, from whatever quarter God speaks.

June 17

The first step of humility is to utterly flee forgetfulness by keeping the fear of God always before one's eyes [Ps 35(36):2]. (RB 7.10)

In the spiritual system of John Cassian, from which Benedict derives his ladder of humility, fear of the Lord is the indispensable precondition for all progress in humility. Although it sounds quite negative and even forbidding to us today, fear of the Lord is a foundational value for the Jewish Bible where it is code language for ideal piety. Many have suggested that "fear" should really be translated as "awe." That is quite helpful, provided we do not thereby open the door to spiritual complacency. In this verse, such complacency is called "forgetfulness" and presented as something to be avoided at all costs. Indeed, the phrase "utterly flee" brings out that idea about as strongly as can be imagined. Perhaps the classic antithesis to fear of the

Lord is the saying of the fool in Psalm 53(54):1: "There is no God" (NAB). This is not a statement of theoretical atheism. It means, I propose to live *as if* there is no God. That is practical atheism, to forget there is a God.

June 18

The seventh step of humility is gained when a monk not only confesses with his tongue, but also believes with all his heart that he is lower and less honorable than all the rest. (RB 7.51)

In our present-day atmosphere of low self-esteem, this passage of the ladder of humility may seem a bit dangerous. Would it not be best to quietly put it aside? But then the ladder would fall down! It is more helpful to revisit the original source, namely, John Cassian's eighth sign of humility. In that text, the point is internalization, not self-abasement. Whatever humility is, it must not remain a mere facade or even a set of behaviors. Rather, it must be deeply felt and become part of one's very consciousness. This is completely in line with Cassian's overall emphasis on internalization. This still leaves us with the problem that many persons in our society seem to suffer from a lack of self-esteem. Yet it is a mark of spiritual and mental health to have a high opinion of those around myself. Let it be written on your tombstone: "She (He) thought the best of everyone unless forced to do otherwise."

Having completed his discourse, the Lord waits every day for us to respond by action to his holy warnings. (RB Prol. 35)

Although taken out of context, this verse closely resembles Matthew 7:28, which is the end of the Sermon on the Mount. Of course, the contents of Prologue 5-34 are different from the Sermon of the Mount, which is much more radical in its demands of the disciple. But the issue is the same: What are you going to do? The Master adds the comment "The Lord is silent," which heightens the dramatic tension. Perhaps Benedict feels he does not need this kind of stage direction. At any rate, what the Lord is waiting for in the Prologue is *action*. Even though there is an important place in the monastic life for reflection and contemplation, the present demand is for implementation. Since permanent commitment seems to be scarce commodity among contemporary young people, this aspect of the Prologue seems particularly relevant in this situation. But beyond that, this verse reminds us that monasticism is primarily a lifestyle, not a philosophy.

June 20

As regards singing and reading, no one should presume to carry out these functions unless he is capable of edifying the listeners. Let that be done with humility, sobriety and reverence, by the one designated by the abbot. (RB 47.3-4)

There are, in fact, many reasons for singing and reading: to express myself, to indoctrinate my hearers, to impress people.

And there are other criteria for appointing singers or readers: to give everyone a chance, to promote self-assurance and so on. None of this seems to count with Benedict. For him, there is only one reason to sing and read: to edify. Now the etymology of edify is revealing, for it means to "build up" or "raise up." In this case, we could say that good reading and singing builds up the community and lifts up the minds and hearts of its members. The means are somewhat different, for singing is primarily about beauty and reading is primarily about intelligibility. But unintelligible singing and ugly reading are also unacceptable. In any case, these are special functions that call for special talents.

June 21

What are [the writings of the Fathers] but tools of virtue for nuns who live uprightly and virtuously? But for us lazy nuns who lead bad and negligent lives, they are a source of embarrassment and shame.
(RB 73.6-7)

"Embarrassment and shame" is *rubor confusionis,* the blush that suffuses the face of many people when they experience acute shame. What is it that occasions this painful reaction in this last chapter of the Rule? The fact that there are wonderful literary helps to spiritual progress available in the Bible and the Fathers—but we do not use them. Benedict calls this condition *desidia*, which is very hard to translate correctly. It does not necessarily mean *physical* laziness, but tepidity toward some value. In this case, it implies a kind of apathy toward growth in holiness, and ultimately toward God. Unfortunately, this condition is not rare among professional religious (nuns and monks) for whom the things of God easily become excessively familiar. If we can just overcome our inertia toward hard spiritual work and apply ourselves to serious *lectio divina,* we do ourselves an enormous favor.

June 22

If anyone arrives at the Night Office after the Gloria of Psalm 94(95) —and for that reason we want it said very slowly and with pauses— he is not to stand in his own place. (RB 43.4)

If there was one thing Father Bede hated, it was tardiness. And coming late to the Night (Morning) Office was even more abhorrent to him. To his mind, such conduct was a sign of a lack of motivation and should be punished according to the rigor of the Rule. He was not satisfied with the enforcement carried out by the superiors. Oh, the latecomers had to "kneel out," but to his mind that was not enough. There should be a special "tardy bench" where they could be a spectacle and warning to all. Yet Bede had to admit that some people could barely get out of bed at 4:30 a.m., much less rush to choir. In fact, he himself was getting old himself and promptness came harder. One day he dragged himself out of bed and hobbled into choir—only to find every single stall empty! At this point, he rushed into the nave of the church and found a novice piously making the Stations of the Cross. "Is it not five o'clock?" shouted Bede. "Yes, yes, it is." "Then why aren't the monks saying Morning Prayer?" "Father, it is five in the afternoon!"

June 23

If the whole community connives to choose a person who will go along with their vices . . . the local bishop or the neighboring prioresses or even the Christians of the district . . . should set a worthy steward over the house of God. (RB 64.3-5)

It sometimes may seem as if the monastery is a sort of separate sphere, but that is not the mentality of the founder. In these surprising verses, Benedict tells the local bishop, prioresses and even the laity, to intervene if the nuns prove that they are incapable of handling their own affairs. The historical reality for most of the history of monasticism in Europe was that kings and governments were only too ready to do so. Indeed, a truly independent monasticism has only been the norm for the past century or so. In that time, it has been rare for the church to feel it necessary to directly impact the affairs of a given monastery. Yet it can happen, and when it does it simply reminds us of a fundamental truth: a monastery is still only a part of the greater church. It is never a world unto itself.

June 24

No one should be excused from kitchen duty. . . . Thus both merit and love are increased. (RB 35.1-2)

Benedict explains his principle that every member be involved in kitchen service (except those who are sick or occupied with essential tasks) by speaking of both merit and love. It is perhaps easier for us to resonate with love than with merit. Mutual service at meals is a privileged biblical form of practical charity, modeled by none other than Jesus himself. But the remark that such service also increases merit may not sit too well with us today. Indeed, the idea of works of mercy leading to heavenly reward is a piece of traditional Christian thinking that has fallen by the wayside. Perhaps we suspect that it leads to a kind of spiritual materialism, or maybe the whole concept was overdeveloped in the old *Baltimore Catechism*. Nonetheless, Jesus himself sometimes promises heavenly rewards to those who obey him, and Benedict is not shy either about speaking of such rewards. It could be that he wants to reassure those who feel that kitchen work is too mundane to count toward spiritual progress. And some may have felt it was beneath them.

June 25

A brother who is judged guilty of serious fault should be banned from both table and oratory. No brother may associate with him or converse with him . . . "A man like that should be given over [to Satan] for fleshly destruction so that his soul may be saved on the day of the Lord" [1 Cor 5:51]. (RB 25.1-2, 4)

Monastic excommunication is not banishment from the sacraments as in the general excommunication of the Church, but it is still dire in its consequences. At least for serious faults, the person is simply ostracized from table and choir. What is more, the other members are strictly forbidden to associate with him. Probably all of this sounds a bit extreme to our modern ears, and perhaps even vaguely unchristian. How can we reconcile this with Jesus' Gospel of forgiveness? The best rebuttal to that argument is found in the fact that Paul himself decreed the very same penalty for a serious sin (incest) in Corinth. But it is still true that in the Christian ethos punishment is not an end in itself. Paul makes the case plainly: chastise the flesh in order to save the soul. If this still seems extreme, we should remember that the stakes here are high—nothing less than life or death.

June 26

Likewise, we will participate in the passion of Christ through patience so as to deserve to be companions with him in his kingdom. Amen. (RB Prol. 50)

This verse is loaded with words beginning with "p," and in Latin there is even one more. Clearly the author, who is not Benedict but the Master, meant to create a memorable utterance. He also made a remarkable theological claim: our patience somehow makes us cooperators in Christ's passion. In our activist culture, patience has a rather passive connotation, so we do not give it a very high place among the virtues. Benedict, however, mentions it many times, and usually in contexts of great significance. Since it implies duration and also other people, it is ideally suited to cenobitic life. Of course, our patience does not save the world from its sins as does the passion of Jesus Christ, but in existential terms it makes life possible for a group of sinners. Given the lifelong commitment of Benedictine monks and nuns, only loving patience enables us to persevere to the end *with each other.* This is not just toleration or passive resignation, it is an intentional engagement in the life of the Body of Christ.

June 27

"Whoever has ears for hearing should listen to what the Spirit says to the churches" [Rev 2:7]. (RB Prol. 11)

This may seem like a commonplace transitional passage to a Scriptural text but it should not be overlooked since it mentions the Spirit. As such it is one of only seven references to the third person of the Holy Trinity to be found in Benedict's Rule. Since the "Lord" (God, Father, Christ) is mentioned over a hundred times, we may say that Benedict's pneumatology is under-developed. But in this he is like most of his contemporaries. Moreover, not much current writing gives the Holy Spirit a prominent place. So it is important for us to keep the Spirit in a central place in our spiritual vision. This is especially true with a patristic text like the Prologue, where the Hebrew Psalms form the bulk of the biblical witness. We are not Old Testament Christians, but persons who believe that the Spirit of Jesus lives in our very hearts. Without the Holy Spirit we are not Christians. It is also a capital mistake to leave the Holy Spirit out of our monastic thinking.

June 28

Pray for your enemies out of love for Christ. (RB 4.72)

When I was a young monk, I scoffed at the idea that a monk could have enemies. Now I think it is the most natural thing in the world. An enemy is someone who has a long-standing antipathy for me, no matter what I may feel about him. Long years in a small, enclosed community have a way of revealing, if not producing, such feelings. At first, and perhaps for years, one is dismayed at this knowledge because one had a more exalted idea of oneself. But eventually you recognize that you are not entirely lovable. Now what to do? There is no "solution" as such, but at least one can *pray* for the other person. But why should I do so? Simply because Christ loves the other one as well as me. What is more, Christ lives somehow in the other one, even if his hatred is not Christ-like. Yet it cannot be denied that knowledge that someone hates me can corrode my attitude toward him. How can I even pray for him? Because Christ lives and prays in me as well.

June 29

"It is good that you humiliate me, so I might learn your commandments" *[Ps 118(119):71].* (RB 7.54)

Benedict embellishes his seventh step of humility with this psalm quote among others. At first glance, it seems unexceptional, especially when we realize that it is meant to bolster the teaching that we should believe others to be better than ourselves. But the word "humiliate" sticks out like a sore thumb. Does God really humiliate anybody? In psychological terms, to humiliate is to deliberately strip away the dignity of another, at least momentarily. Now, it is hard to reconcile this with the activity of a loving God such as we believe in. Yet we might make a distinction between the intention and the result of such an action. It is quite possible that when I get what I deserve, or when I experience the burden of my creaturehood as particularly heavy, I *feel* humiliated by God. Perhaps all of this uneasiness could have been avoided if the translator had just rendered the verb "humbled." At any rate, we must still insist that no one is justified in humiliating another in the name of religion.

June 30

Above all, the evil of murmuring must not appear for any reason,
by any word or gesture whatsoever. If anyone is caught at this,
he should undergo a severe punishment. (RB 34.6)

Benedict does not like "murmuring." This may puzzle the
modern reader, who thinks it just means a continuous low
sound. But for Benedict it means complaining, and he cannot
stand it. That may be a quirk of his character, but this particular passage gives us a rare insight into the background of the
theme. In chapter 34, the monks are warned against a specific
kind of envy. Even though they have personally had their needs
met, they complain because others have received more. It is a
particular kind of ingratitude that is fueled by wants and not
needs. In the Bible, a comparable situation arises in the Desert
of Sinai where the Israelites "murmur" (Latin, *murmurare*)
against Moses and God for leading them out to die of thirst
and hunger. All they can remember are the leeks and onions of
Egypt. What they forget is that they have been liberated by
God from Egyptian slavery. Seen in this light, murmuring
about material slights can be seen as symbolic of our lack of
gratitude for God's saving grace to us.

July 1

Idleness is the soul's enemy, so therefore at determined times the
brothers ought to be occupied with manual labor, and again at
determined times in lectio divina. (RB 48.1)

Benedict likes to begin his chapters with memorable aphorisms and this is certainly one of those instances. Since it is

often invoked to show that Benedict promotes hard work, it must appeal to many of his modern readers. But it would be a mistake, I think, to call it one of his basic principles. It is true that he also repeats this idea in the last verses of this chapter. But a comparison with chapter 50 of the Rule of the Master, which is on the same subject, clearly shows that Benedict has toned down the importance of work. In his elaborate horarium, the Master shows that he equates idleness with sin. Thus it is not surprising when he attempts to fill every possible minute with activity. But in fact overwork is just as inimical to the soul as idleness, and it is something that many people in our society are suffering right now. Despite appearances, Benedict seems to allow his monks enough free time for them to exercise their freedom as the sons of God. Without freedom there is no contemplation.

July 2

Holy Father Basil. (RB 73.5)

Why does Benedict call Basil "holy father"? Is this merely a *topos*, a kind of pious cliché, not to be taken too literally? When we look into the matter more closely, we note that Basil certainly isn't one of the main literary sources of Benedict. If one is to count explicit references, that honor belongs to the Rule of the Master, then Cassian, then Augustine. And of course, Basil is a Greek "church father" whom Benedict could only have read in the Latin translation. But this need not rule out Benedict's dependency on Basil. It is plausible to locate the linchpin of Benedict' spirituality in the first degree of humility, where he teaches that the whole monastic life is based on the fear of the Lord. For Benedict, this means primarily that the nun is constantly aware of God and also convinced that God is aware of her. Since this same theme is enunciated no less than four times in the Rule, it seems to be central. Now, the language and concepts employed in those passages come from the writings of Basil. And so perhaps we can take Benedict's formula "Holy Father Basil" rather literally.

July 3

He must stand in the last place or in a place which the abbot has set apart for those who err in this way [by coming late]. (RB 43.5)

In the old regime, those who came late to choir had to "kneel out." This meant flopping down in the sanctuary and praying the Our Father, Hail Mary and Glory Be silently before proceeding to one's choir stall.

One nasty feature of kneeling out at St. James Abbey was that one had to do it right in front of the abbot's throne. But the shame had worn off long ago for Father Brian; he was a chronic latecomer. No matter how much he wanted to be on time, and no matter how vigorously he resolved to come on time, he just couldn't do it. He knew that Benedict takes a dim view of this fault, but he did not know how to overcome it. Sometimes in private interviews, the abbot would make practical suggestions: start earlier, plan your work more carefully, get to one thing on time and maybe all the rest will follow. Brian tried all these tricks, but nothing worked. One day, however, things did fall into place. He actually came to Morning Prayer on time. But since he was so used to coming late, he automatically knelt out and said his prayers. "Go to your place, Brian, you are on time!" hissed the abbot.

July 4

The prioress must be learned in the Divine Law so that she will know how to "bring forth both old things and new" [Matt 13:52]. (RB 64.9)

"Divine Law" here refers to the Bible, not canon law. Benedict wants his superior to be very familiar with the Scriptures, not just to be learned but to feed the community. Traditionally, not many American superiors have felt capable of filling this role and many of them simply did not try. But there really is no excuse for this at all. Obviously, not every prioress can be a biblical scholar. But every prioress can study and pray over the Bible, and she can share her *lectio* with the community. The idea of "both old things and new" could refer to the need for both exegesis and hermeneutics. That is, one needs to study the ancient text as carefully as possible; but then one must take the next step: What does this mean for us right now, right here? None of this suggests that a Benedictine community should be a gathering of scholars. Yet it should indeed be gathered around the Bible, and that book ought to be its primary text.

July 5

The weak should be provided help in (kitchen) work so they do not lose heart. In fact, all should have help, according to the size of the community and the local circumstances. (RB 35.3-4)

Here is an example of Benedict's utterly practical approach to charity. Like the good Roman he is, his mind runs in very down-to-earth channels. The principle set out here is so obvious as to seem beneath comment: people must have the help they need to do their job. The alternative is to leave them in positions that are untenable. Of course, the weak *(imbecillitas)* will need help more than anyone else almost by definition. It is a form of cruel neglect to fail to give them help. But other kinds of people also suffer acutely from lack of sufficient help. Perfectionists, of which monasteries are typically well-stocked, seem to experience a special kind of anguish when they do not have the means to do their work well. Others take a more philosophical attitude: if they don't give me adequate help, then they can't expect much in return. But it can happen that "they" simply don't have the personnel to send to the rescue.

July 6

The abbot should focus all his attention on the case of wayward brothers, for "it is not the healthy but the sick who need a physician" [Matt 9:12]. (RB 27.1)

The title for chapter 27 is translated "The Abbot's Preoccupation *(sollicitus)* with the Excommunicated." Some might consider that an example of "over-interpretation," but the contents of the chapter seem to bear it out. Here toward the end of Benedict's "penal code" is a poignant little treatise on how the abbot should relate to a monk who must be excommunicated. In short, he must concern himself with little else!

One time after an abbatial election, one of the monks on mission, before returning to his parish, said to an "at home" monk: "If the new abbot starts running this place like General Motors, stand up on your hind legs and bark like hell!"

Whatever else goes on at General Motors, it is clear that they do not concentrate all their attention on one troubled employee. That just isn't an efficient way to operate, but who ever said that monastic community life was about efficiency? Like it or not, the abbot's ministry is like that of Jesus to those who "labor and are burdened" (Matt 11:28; NAB).

July 7

Likewise, we will participate in the passion of Christ through patience so as to deserve to be companions with him in his kingdom. Amen. (RB Prol. 50)

In this verse, Benedict is copying from the Rule of the Master. For the Master, the "school for the Lord's service" is primarily a school of suffering with Christ. This harsh spirituality is worked out in practical detail in this rather strange monastic Rule, but at the very end of the Prologue the Master relieves the tension by showing that its goal is heaven. The Master then goes on to paint a rather sensuous, even lurid, picture of heaven (which Benedict omits). But in this verse, the Master describes heaven in more personal terms: it is the place where we will be companions with Christ. This in turn may reflect the early Christian spirituality of martyrdom, in which the martyr typically is sustained by personal love for Christ. From that perspective, the passion of Christ is not an abstraction, but a devastating experience in the life of someone we love. The same awareness can help us to live a life of faithful patience in this life, with the fervent hope that we will spend eternity with our Beloved.

And what does the Spirit say? "Come, children, and hear me; I will teach you the fear of the Lord" [Ps 33(34):12]. (RB Prol. 12)

This is the way Benedict, following the Master, begins his commentary on Psalm 33(34) in the Prologue. It may surprise and even disappoint us to hear that this is what the Spirit has to say to us! Surely the Spirit of Jesus could teach us something more fruitful than the fear of the Lord? In truth, fear, any kind of fear, is distasteful to modern persons and we are hesitant to associate it with religion. Many people describe their problems with organized religion as a question of fear: they object to being bullied into heaven. Sad to say, this casts a pall on a perfectly good Jewish concept, the fear of the Lord. A casual search through the Jewish Bible reveals that this was in fact the chief characteristic of the truly pious Jew: fear of the Lord. And there is no evidence to show that Jesus repudiated this language. Even though he often used the intimate term *abba* (dad) toward his Father, all of his teaching inculcates religious awe toward God.

If we have plied [the tools of the spiritual craft] ceaselessly day and night, and returned them on Judgment Day, we will receive that reward from the Lord which he promised. (RB 4.76)

The image of returning tools after their use may seem to reinforce Benedict's reputation for teaching the sanctity of work. But in fact the "work" of Benedict's monk is all the spiritual effort listed in chapter 4. Indeed, the "work" of the monk is progress in the spiritual life itself; anything else is "in addition." The idea of receiving a "reward" may strike some as a kind of spiritual materialism and not worthy of a mature personality. Nevertheless, the New Testament reports that Jesus himself promised "rewards" to those who follow him (Matt 5:12). And this is not the only time Benedict speaks of merit and heavenly reward. Those who lived through an age of "merit theology" have reason to be wary of this language, but they should also remember that "the best is the enemy of the good." In other words, an excessively high standard may undermine even a moderate norm and end by leaving nothing.

July 10

Let [the cellarer] not be motivated by greed, nor should he waste or squander the goods of the monastery. But he should do everything with moderation and according to the abbot's directives. (RB 31.12)

It is clear that one of the cellarer's most important attributes must be "moderation" or balance. By this means alone will he be able to steer a proper course between stinginess and prodigality. Not everyone is endowed with this kind of level-headedness. A lot depends on our home background and other factors over which we have no control. But as someone remarked, "avarice seems to be the besetting sin of the twenty-first century." I take that to mean that everything is now decided on the basis of money. Given this imbalance, it is not unusual to find veteran monks, and holy ones, who are not well balanced when it comes to material things. But it must be admitted that it is not an easy matter to know exactly where, in a given situation, the happy mean is in fact located. In fact, economic questions in modern times are notoriously obscure and convoluted. Sometimes mere common sense is no longer enough. A cellarer today must try to know where economic moderation *really* lies.

July 11

From Easter till the first of October, they should go out from prime in the morning and work until almost the fourth hour at what is necessary. But from the fourth hour until the time they recite Sext, they should be free for lectio divina. (RB 48.3-4)

This short excerpt from chapter 48 gives us the essence of Benedict's horarium. Apart from the liturgy, the monks are to occupy themselves in one of two ways: either by manual work or by *lectio divina.* Overall, they are to spend about six hours at work and three hours in *lectio.* We know all about work, but do we know about *lectio divina?* A literal translation of this word might be "spiritual reading," but that could be misleading. The early monks did not consider just any pious book the proper object of *lectio divina.* For them, it meant engagement with the Bible. This could involve memorization of the text for later "meditation" (rumination). *Lectio divina* was not simple bible study as we know it; it was closer to prayer. That the ancient monks spent a great deal of time with the Bible is evident in everything they wrote. Not only do they quote the Bible extensively, their very language is saturated with the diction of Scripture.

July 12

And then there are the Conferences *of the Fathers and their* Institutes *and* Lives, *along with the Rule of our Holy Father Basil.* (RB 73.5)

Almost all commentators agree that the *Conferences* and *Institutes* mentioned here refer to John Cassian, for they are the titles of the two main bodies of his works. The *Lives* of the Fathers probably refers to the Egyptian work of that title, which had been translated shortly before Benedict's time. If Cassian is indeed the reference, then the yoking of him with Basil is worth noting. For Cassian promotes the anchoretic life and Basil is wholly interested in the cenobitic form of monasticism. For Benedict to claim that *both* of these authors provide important *lectio divina* for his monks tells us a lot about the mentality of the Italian abbot. He is a not a one-dimensional fanatic. He knows that the rich reality of monastic life has many facets. So, as Michael Casey has remarked, the Rule of Benedict itself is a kind of "earthquake-proof building," because it is an amalgam of both kinds of thinking. It is a special sign of maturity to be able to entertain a range of ideas without having to exclude anything before due consideration.

July 13

Do not be habitually quarrelsome. (RB 4.68)

According to the former canon law, it is an especially grave sin to do bodily harm to a religious. In fact, it results in excommunication.

At least that is what Brother Bert told Brother Wolfgang one day when the latter was on the point of beating him senseless.

To make it even more impressive, Bert said that only the abbot could forgive such a sin. To do so, he would have to dress up in full pontificals and he would use a book, bell and candle. These two little lay brothers worked together in the cow barn, but they never got along. Bert was stubborn and pugnacious, while Wolfgang was mild and easygoing. But he had his limits. One day Bert actually stuck his chin way out and dared Wolfie to punch him. At that point Wolfgang lost all control and knocked Bert unconscious. Then he marched up the hill to the monastery. When he got there, he flung open the back door and cried out "Get the abbot! I just knocked out Brother Bert!"

July 14

The abbot must indeed exercise very great care, and hasten with all keenness and energy to prevent any of the sheep entrusted to him from being lost. (RB 27.5)

It was a worst-case scenario. Father Peter had not only disgraced himself in his parish with his drinking; he had become a *fugitivus* by leaving the system altogether. His next move was to drive a cab in a nearby town, which infuriated Abbot Oscar. Then he worked on the railroad section crew as a gandy dancer. At least this took him far away from the monastery, which was what the abbot wanted. Although the Abbot felt profound sadness at Father Peter's collapse, he was not surprised by it. No matter what he had done, he could never bring the monk under discipline and he had simply ruined himself. Hence Oscar was not very pleased when he received a letter from Abbot Ildephonse of St. Stephen's Abbey, informing him that Peter had shown up at the door; could he take him in? "I have half a mind to deny permission!" said Oscar to the young prior, Father Paschal, who stood before his desk. "Then I would not want to be standing in your place come Judgment Day, Father Abbot" said Paschal.

July 15

Local conditions may be such that even the amount of wine mentioned above [one hemina] cannot be had, but much less or none at all. Then those who live there should bless God and not murmur. Most of all, we warn them to avoid murmuring. (RB 40.8-9)

Coming at the end of the chapter on the consumption of wine, this may seem to be a kind of gratuitous detail. Yet in a way it is more important than the main subject of the chapter. The comment may refer to a wide geographical area, or it may simply refer to the vagaries of the grape harvest. Thus for example, there are no wine grapes grown in England; and there may be a rare year when none can be harvested in some section of Italy. Whatever the context, there is still an important a principle at stake: people should refrain from grumbling about the conditions of their lives, and that especially pertains to monks. Although this chapter discusses the rather heroic asceticism of abstaining from wine (in the Mediterranean zone), there is a deeper asceticism that consists of accepting cheerfully whatever life presents. The latter is a far more demanding discipline that does not involve penance of our own choosing.

July 16

[The abbot] should use all the methods known to a wise physician. For example, he can send in senpectae, that is, wise, elderly brothers who know how to console the wavering brother, as if in secret. (RB 27.2-3)

The scenario here is excommunication. A brother has been ostracized, but the penalty has not been effective. He will not repent, he will not change his ways. What to do? At this point, Benedict exhibits a degree of psychological cleverness equal to his reputation. Instead of attempting to bulldoze the miscreant into submission, the abbot should step aside and send in mediators. That in itself implies humility on the part of the abbot. Whatever *senpectae* means, it is clear that these go-betweens are not exactly part of the power-structure. Rather, they are "wise, elderly," that is, non-threatening. Beyond that we find the intriguing phrase "as if in secret" *(quasi secrete)*. Are they to pretend they are breaking the Rule by fraternizing without the abbot's orders? Surely not. No doubt they make sure the whole affair is carried out without fanfare. At any rate, they must be careful to uphold *both* justice and mercy. That is, they urge repentance, but they also offer consolation.

July 17

The eighth step of humility is when a monk does nothing except what is encouraged by the common rule of the monastery and the example of its veteran members. (RB 7.55)

Taken at face value, this maxim seems to promote the most intransigent form of social conservatism. In such a system, how could a new idea ever make its way in, or how could necessary change ever be effected? The rubbish heap of history is strewn with the husks of institutions that could not or would not change. On the other hand, it must be remembered that a given monastery is a human organism that usually can only change gradually. In fact, all traditional societies are heavily based on continuity rather than innovation.

Before Brother Bede attended his first chapter meeting, Father Dismas half-joked to him: "New chapter members should probably not speak for the first ten years." This kind of attitude can be frustrating to some persons but it is important that they do not throw up their hands and give up too soon. The group needs the fresh ideas and energy of the newcomer.

July 18

The first kind [of monks] are the cenobites, who live in monasteries and serve under a rule and an abbot. (RB 1.2)

This chapter, which is taken almost verbatim from the Rule of the Master, serves as a kind of author's preface, in which he first defines his subject, the cenobites. The claim that they "live in monasteries" is not too helpful, since anchorites also do that. John Cassian, who also presents a taxonomy of "kinds of monks" (*Conf.* 18.4), says that cenobites "live together in a community." Benedict never uses the word "cenobite" after chapter 1, but it is clear that he has a very high opinion of community. The pair "rule and abbot" seems to be equal, but in fact it is not. One clue is that the order is never reversed when it is found in the Rule of St. Benedict. That is because the abbot also lives "under a rule." Historically speaking, the founder of a monastery often serves as the virtual embodiment of the Rule. But when the leadership is passed on to a successor, a written Rule becomes necessary. The verb here translated "serve" is *militans,* which literally means "fight." This chapter emphasizes the monastic life as hard struggle *(ascesis).*

July 19

Run while you have the light of life, that the darkness not overtake you [John 12:23]. (RB Prol. 13)

Since the preceding verse spoke of the "fear of the Lord," it would appear that the Master and Benedict see this fear as associated with evil and death: if we do not flee to the Lord we will be swallowed up by destruction. In order to make this point as urgently as possible, they have not hesitated to heighten the language of John 12:35. "Walk" is changed to "run" and there is the addition of "life" and "death." Clearly, they mean to communicate the spiritual journey as a life and death flight that allows no dawdling. In fact, the verb "run" occurs often in the Rule of St. Benedict and at strategic points in the Prologue itself. It is hardly to be taken literally, since monks cannot be expected to be running around like young chickens. But it symbolizes eagerness and spiritual alacrity; its antithesis is sloth and a lack of energy for the things of God. The Prologue wishes to insist to the candidate that the time is short; one must put the remaining time to the best use possible.

July 20

We will receive that reward from the Lord which he promised: "What eye has not seen nor ear heard, God has prepared for those who love him" [1 Cor 2:9]. (RB 4.76-77)

Coming as it does at the end of chapter 4, "What Are the Tools of Good Works?" this promise of heavenly reward is not at first glance so remarkable. But source criticism shows that

Benedict has written it to replace a very long and lurid description of heaven in the Rule of the Master. Although that passage has a sort of naive charm, Benedict apparently considers it to be essentially a distraction that needs to be set aside. Instead he opts for one of the most beautiful, evocative verses in the New Testament. For all his theological depth, Paul knows that he does not know much about heaven. He does know that it will utterly surpass anything on earth we might compare to it. But it is also true that the essential content of heaven is God himself, the reward of rewards. Benedict knows that, too, and so we can say that he is replacing the materialist heaven of the Master with a deeply personal concept.

July 21

Let us give "praise" to our Creator for "his deeds of justice"
[Ps 118 (119):164] at the following times: Matins, Prime, Terce, Sext,
None, Vespers and Compline. And "Let us rise at night to praise him"
[Ps 118(119):62]. (RB 16.5)

Chapter 16 of the Rule is mainly addressed to the question: how many times should we pray each day? For the old monks, this was a burning question because they thought of themselves precisely as those Christians who took literally the injunction of Paul to "pray always" (1 Thess 5:17). John Cassian (*Inst.* 3.1-3) thought it was a mistake to even attempt to fulfill this biblical command by set offices, but it would seem that cenobites have no other option. Life on planet earth requires that some time be given to tasks like eating, working, sleeping and so forth. So the monks try to space their prayer periods throughout the day. What should we pray for? Benedict wants us to praise God for his deeds of justice. That would seem to place us in the category of creation spirituality, where the emphasis lies in acknowledging God's overwhelming goodness in creating and sustaining the world. Next we must ask, what we can do to help?

July 22

One or two seniors should surely be assigned to patrol the monastery at the times when the brothers are free for lectio. *They should be on the lookout for the bored brother who gives himself over to frivolity or gossip and is not serious about* lectio . . . *Nor should the brothers fraternize at improper times.* (RB 48.17-18, 21)

In chapter 48, Benedict provides his monks with three daily hours in which to perform *lectio divina*. More precisely, he says they are "free for" *(vacant) lectio*. Given that evocative language, we might be taken aback by the fact that some of them appear to have found *lectio* hard, so hard they preferred to do other things like gossip. This paradox, that *lectio* should be both liberating and hard, can tell us much about it. One reason that *lectio divina* is hard is because the Bible is not always easy to understand. But the problem runs deeper than this. Biblical prayer is a doorway to contemplation of God, but that invariably involves confrontation with ourselves. Compared to the Holy One, we get a clearer notion of our own unholiness. *Lectio divina* is not easy because growth in the Spirit is never easy.

July 23

What book of the Holy Catholic Fathers does not teach us how to arrive at our Creator by the direct route? (RB 73.4)

As with the previous verse, the claim here is that a certain kind of reading will guide us directly toward God and our eternal salvation. In verse 73.3 it was the Bible, and now it is the Holy Catholic Fathers. Benedict does not say exactly who these writers are, but we could say that he is simply referring to authentic Catholic tradition. But that may just push the question back one notch. Probably he wants to make sure his monks were not reading Arian tracts, for in the sixth century Italy was overrun by the Goths, who were Arian (non-orthodox) Christians. After fifteen hundred years, no doubt the deposit of Catholic tradition is a good deal more ample than in the time of Benedict. Still, it is a good idea for Benedictines to stay in close touch with the same church fathers to whom Benedict here refers. There is something bracing and essentially nourishing about their piety that seems more germane to us than the latest devotion, no matter how attractive.

July 24

When someone comes first to the monastic life, he should not be allowed entry too readily. (RB 58.1)

Henry was looking for Father Rudolf. He had come out to the abbey from Minnesota at the urging of his friend, Chuck, who was a student. Both of them hoped to eventually join the novitiate. "When you get here, look for Father Rudy," wrote

Chuck. So after Henry got off the train and walked up to the monastery, he immediately asked for Rudy. "He's out at the football field," said the student he first met. That pleased Henry, who was himself a stellar athlete. But when he got to the football field, he could see no monks. In fact, there was at least one monk there, since Rudy was on the field scrimmaging with the students. Since he was not wearing a habit, however, Henry could not distinguish him. Finally, he did see an old monk standing on the far side of the field, watching the action. Thinking he must be Father Rudolf, Henry made his way to him and introduced himself. "Hi, Father! I'm Henry Fairchild from Red Lake, Minnesota!" "So what?" said Father Benno.

July 25

Paying attention to these and other passages that praise discretion, the mother of virtues, the prioress should arrange everything to challenge the bold, not to overwhelm the timid. (RB 64.19)

In calling for balance and discretion in his prioress, Benedict is drawing from the wells of Christian wisdom. It is true that brilliant, mercurial people are needed to imagine and drive great projects. And there are times when qualities such as courage are perhaps as important as discretion. But by and large, the top authority in a human community has to have a large amount of discretion. Yet we are not talking here about just *any* community, but a Christian monastery. So this must be that special Christian form of discretion that draws on the divine sources for its inspiration. Indispensable as they are, simple common sense and prudence are not enough. The discretion of the Holy Spirit, especially speaking through the Scriptures, is needed. Otherwise, we will just be operating by the principles of the world, and not of God. Finally, in every community, the main job of the leader is to keep everyone working at the same values and goals. "No nun left behind!"

July 26

The blessing of obedience is not only something all the sisters should render to the prioress, but to each other as well. Therefore, except for the orders of the prioress or the officials she has appointed, which we allow no private commands to override, all juniors must obey their seniors with every mark of loving attention. (RB 71.1, 3-4)

A sharp reader may suspect that the translator has nodded on this one. How does the second sentence follow logically from the first? In fact, the second contradicts the first, and the illogicality is Benedict's not mine! But these kinds of slips can sometimes tell us more about an author than when he is in complete control. It is obvious that Benedict is not comfortable with mutual obedience. He begins to expound it with great panache, but within a few lines he veers off into the "exception," namely, hierarchical obedience, which is what he really loves. That becomes the main topic of this rather unbalanced chapter. And yet Benedict *will* exult in mutual obedience in the next chapter. Perhaps we have here a precious glimpse of his stumbling toward that hard doctrine? I find it edifying to see that even the great ones arrive at truth by tortuous paths.

July 27

He can send in senpectae, that is, wise, elderly brothers who know how to console the wavering brother, as if in secret. (RB 27.3)

Father Wally had burned his bridges. He had been ordered by Abbot Ronald to move from St. Pius to Round Lake, but he refused to do so. The diocese had decided to close rural St. Pius and Wally was so distraught that he even called the local newspaper and told them he wasn't going to budge. They would have to evict him with dynamite! His housekeeper was more level-headed, knowing that you can't fight city hall, much less both the abbot and the bishop. When the phone rang, it wasn't the abbot but the prior of the monastery, Father Aidan. "Hi Wally. How are you?" "Oh fine, just fine." "Mind if I come out and visit you?" "No. No. I would be happy to see you. We don't see too many visitors out here." Wally was pretty relieved. Aidan was a nice guy, considered by everyone to be one of the gentlest monks in the monastery. He liked him much better than the bombastic abbot. The next week he quietly moved to Round Lake without informing the newspaper.

July 28

The ninth step of humility comes when a monk restrains his tongue from speaking, and out of love for silence does not speak until he is asked a question. (RB 7.56)

The ninth step of humility is as radical as any of the other steps of Benedict's ladder of humility, but it is doubtful whether any Benedictine monastery has ever carried it out to the letter. Actually, it looks like a remnant of the Master's elaborate doctrine of silence (RM 8–9) which does not permit "perfect disciples" to initiate a conversation, at least with the abbot. One forum where this ethos still prevails is the monastic chapter meeting, where the abbot sets the agenda and no one can speak unless bidden. But in general the Benedictine monk enjoys the *parrhesia* (freedom of speech) of the children of God. Yet there is still something spiritually beneficial about restraining one's speech, especially if one does it not out of fear of censure but out of love for silence itself. In fact, mandatory silence has a very different quality from that which proceeds from love. In the latter case, persons have internalized a basic monastic value: they do not just "keep quiet," they *are* quiet.

July 29

The second kind are the anchorites, that is, hermits. Their observance is no mere novice fervor, but the result of long testing in a monastery.
(RB 1.3)

Chapter 1 insists that it is dangerous to become a monastic hermit without first being trained in a monastic community. From the standpoint of ordinary psychology and common sense, this is no doubt true. But it is also true that many great monastic hermits had no such experience in a cenobium. Furthermore, there are unfortunate corollaries to this theory. For one thing, it implies that the hermit is *superior* to the cenobite by definition. That is a claim that many monastic writers seem to assume, but which is fiercely resisted by the great cenobitic writer, Basil of Caesarea (Latin Rule 3). What is more, it tends to make of the cenobium a mere training school for hermits, which it is not. At its finest, the cenobitic community is not an instrument or means to something else, but itself a "perfect" Christian structure. Yet apart from this caveat, it is still true that someone who wishes to pursue a solitary monastic existence needs to submit to the salutary "testing" of the church.

The Lord, seeking a worker for himself in the crowds, again cries out: "Which of you desires life and longs to see good days?" [Ps 33(34):13]. (RB Prol. 14-15)

Here the psalm verse is introduced by the concrete image of God as a landowner or a construction foreman, hiring day laborers in the marketplace. The Bible contains several such passages, whether in the parable of the vineyard workers (Matt 20:1-16) or that of Wisdom (Prov 8 and 9). We notice here that the one hiring does not merely issue a curt summons: "Come and work!" Rather, he entices the potential worker with an attractive offer, indeed, the most attractive offer possible; "life and good days." Who could resist such an offer? There are passages in Benedict's Rule that rebuff and all but reject the newcomer (for example, 58.1-3), but if we believe that the Christian, monastic life truly *does* offer "life and good days," then it is hard to see how we can fail to invite others to share it. Moreover, this is much more than a mere labor recruitment. Here God is inviting others to work *with* him. This is a true vocation call.

July 31

Through the example and support of the community, (the anchorites) have learned to fight the devil. This excellent training in the fraternal battle line equips them to venture out to the desert for solo combat. (RB 1.4-5)

Although not many people nowadays think of the monastic life as a fight against the devil, that was not true of the ancient monks. In fact, the earliest written monastic life, namely, the *Life of Antony* by Athanasius, presents that Egyptian hermit as *primarily* a warrior against the demons. Whether we choose to interpret that battle in realistic or psychological terms, it occupies most of Antony's time, at least for the first years of his monastic life. The Rule of the Master claims that the evil one attacks the monk more fiercely than the layperson, because he fears that he has lost one of his disciples. After this chapter, which is lifted verbatim from the Master, Benedict does not spend much time talking about the devil. But apparently he agrees with the proposition that the anchoritic war with the demons is much more dangerous because it is carried on alone. This is not to suggest that the anchorite should try to carry on without spiritual direction. But the best defense against self-delusion is probably the honest mutual criticism of cenobitic life.

August 1

The workshop where we should accomplish this work is the monastic enclosure and stability in the community. (RB 4.78)

This last verse of the chapter "What Are the Tools of Good Works?" matches the concrete imagery of the title itself. One often uses tools in a workshop. As an abstract noun, stability is not an exact match for the monastic enclosure, but Benedict probably means stability in the monastery. On first glance, we might feel that these concrete images are not exactly appropriate for a spiritual topic. Still, it must be insisted that, for all its spiritual dimensions, monastic life itself has an indispensable concrete dimension. To put it another way, monastic life is not just spiritual feeling but practical lifestyle. Actually, the mention of "community" reinforces this down-to-earth aspect of cenobitic life: it is life with a certain group of people, not an ideal community. As a gruff, old Benedictine abbot once remarked: "I have been dealt a certain hand (of monks) and let me tell you, they ain't all aces!" To remain with a given group year after year, struggling along with them to do God's will, this gives Benedictine life a solid, realistic quality.

August 2

A nun may not receive letters, pious gifts or little presents from her family or anybody else without permission of the prioress. If she orders that it be accepted, the prioress still has the right to give it to whom she chooses. (RB 54.1, 3)

There are things in the Rule of Benedict that probably strike the lay reader as absurd. Some of these things also strike some nuns the same way. Nevertheless, there they are in the Rule, and they are not just an embarrassment but something to be faithfully struggled with. To prohibit the free exchange of presents between a nun and her family seems rather inhumane, yet we should remember that ancient families were usually much more powerful and possessive than our modern ones. They did not gladly give up a child to the monastery, and even after she became a nun, they tried for dear life to hold on to her. Modern parents sometimes find more subtle means to maintain control. Ideally, the mature nun will arrive at a place where she does not need little presents from anybody to be happy and fulfilled. If the prioress should be so foolish as to redistribute the presents, it would make no great difference to her.

August 3

If the necessities of the place or poverty demand that they themselves work at the harvest, they should not be sad. For if they live by the work of their hands, then they are true monks, as were our fathers and the apostles. (RB 48.7-8)

Most modern monks accept the idea that they should earn their bread through work, if not by manual labor. But before we become too enthusiastic about "monks and work," we should try to think clearly about the issue. Is it really true that work really makes the monk? If so, then the monks of St. Martin of Tours were not monks, because they deliberately avoided physical work. As for the apostles, it is true that the Gospels describe them as fishermen, tax-collectors and so forth. But they are rarely shown actually working, nor does the New Testament often claim that work is integral to a Christian life. Still, it is hard to see how monks can practice "poverty" without working. And it is also a truism of psychology that satisfying work is a big contributor to mental health. American monks and nuns have usually been hardworking, but we have not been as adept with the contemplative dimension of our monastic life.

August 4

For what page or even what single word of the divinely inspired Old and New Testaments is not a completely reliable guidepost for human life? (RB 73.3)

A statement like this may seem excessive to us, who surely do find some parts of the Bible difficult to appreciate. Yet the early Christian did not feel this way; indeed, they almost seem to seek out the least attractive parts of the Bible, such as the Book of Leviticus, for material for their *lectio divina*. They were looking for Christ in every line of the Scripture, and they found him. Their exegetical methods might seem quaint to us at times, but there is no doubt that they were completely committed to the Bible. Further, in chapter 73, Benedict wants to make sure that we understand that his "little" Rule is by no means the chief text for his followers. The main text is the Bible itself, for which the Rule is but an interpretive tool. Some monastic Rules, such as that of Basil, consist of little but biblical commentary. As for Benedict, his use of the Scripture is less formal, but almost every chapter of the Rule is saturated with biblical overtones.

August 5

If a nobleman wishes to offer his daughter to God in the monastery, and if she has not reached her majority, the parents themselves should prepare the petition. They should wrap the petition and the girl's hand along with the Mass oblation in the altar cloth, and offer her in this way. (RB 59.1-2)

We could quietly expunge these verses from the Holy Rule, but there would a loss in doing so. For they speak of a time when parents sometimes felt such gratitude to God for a child that they gave her back to God. That is a heartbreaking, stunning possibility that is unthinkable in our society. Why? Besides our lack of faith, there is also the matter of freedom of choice. We passionately believe that each person has a fundamental right to choose her own path. And it should also be noted that the historical record of child oblation was not edifying. Too often rich parents put girls in convents because they could not afford the dowries to marry them off. The poor need not apply.

August 6

It has often happened that the appointment of a subprioress has caused grave scandals to arise in monasteries. There are some who become puffed up with an evil spirit of pride, considering themselves second prioresses and grasping at tyrannical power. (RB 65.1-2)

Chapter 65 is a very troubled chapter, a real anomaly in a Rule that is famous for its balance. This chapter is not balanced! It is furiously agitated and angry about some things. Some scholars have attempted to take Benedict off the hook by suggesting that someone else wrote this chapter. Hardly. Benedict is quite capable of flying off the handle. We really do not know what has prejudiced him against the idea of a prior. Other sources from the sixth century show that officials such as Gregory the Great routinely appointed both prioress and subprioress. We have no report that this caused problems. As for subprioresses, large monasteries have always had them and they are indispensable. Of course, we can accept the general maxim that a subprioress who fancies herself as great as the prioress ("a second prioress") is a serious problem in the monastery. Benedict seems especially leery of a power struggle in his monastery. It is a gross violation of monastic humility.

August 7

Let each one propose to his abbot what he wishes to offer to God [during Lent] so that it is done with his blessing and approval. (RB 49.8)

It was a yearly chore that Brother Philip did not relish. Besides the considerable penance of fast and abstinence during Lent, each monk was expected to offer something personal and special. They had to bring a short list to the abbot's office, where he would read it out loud and then deposit it in a sealed jar with his blessing. Philip could never think of anything to do for penance. Furthermore, the abbot was known to make sharp remarks about the lists; sometimes he demanded that they be changed or discarded altogether. Not only that—Philip was not known as a particularly regular monk. He had his own regimen, and it didn't always coincide with that of the rest of the brotherhood. He and the abbot had clashed over this many times. Still, Philip wanted to make a good impression, so he wrote: "1. Give up snuff. 2. Give up candy. 3. Give up toothpicks." "Why don't you just come to Morning Office?" said the abbot.

August 8

The abbot certainly must exercise very great care, and hasten [race] with all keenness and energy to prevent the loss of any of the sheep in his charge. (RB 27.5-6)

At this point in chapter 27, Benedict shifts from the image of the abbot as physician to abbot as shepherd. Both have biblical roots, but the shepherd is much more prominent in Scripture. If we take a realistic look at this image, we may have to change our idea of the abbot. Herding sheep is not an easy job. It is a job for a young person—or at least one who is willing to undergo all kinds of hardships to protect and nurture the sheep. Nothing could be farther removed from this than the image of a pompous prelate sitting on his throne, bossing people around. This is a job where dignity is a very low priority; all that counts is the welfare of the sheep. Although it is hard to make it work here, a strong translation of *currere* such as "race" is in place since that is what one does to rescue a loved one from disaster.

August 9

The tenth step of humility consists in not being quick to laugh at everything, for it is written: "The fool raises his voice in laughter" [Prov 21:23]. (RB 7.59)

St. Benedict has often been accused of lacking a sense of humor. It is not certain that he would mind such criticism, but most modern persons would. In our society, a sense of humor is virtually a trademark for good mental health. What is criticized in this tenth step of humility, however, is not mirth but raucous humor. In the ancient mentality, that went together with ribaldry. Indeed, some modern commentators suspect that Benedict's censure of loud laughter is really code language for a prohibition of homosexual behavior among his monks! That seems questionable, but what is beyond doubt is the value of good humor in a cenobitic community. Conversely, there is nothing that weighs more heavily on such a group than the habitually morose person. While clinical depression needs to be approached professionally, at least there must be no glorification of glum looks and foul moods. Still, some people are not endowed with a good sense of humor and they make fools of themselves by forced attempts at good cheer.

August 10

[In the desert, the anchorites] are able to fight with God's help against vices of body and mind, relying on their own strength rather than on the support of others. (RB 1.5)

This reference to the desert monastic spirituality of the East has encouraged many commentators to assume that this spirituality is one of Benedict's main inspirations. It must be remembered that he is quoting here from the Rule of the Master, which plainly admires that monastic model. In fact, the Master pursues the master-disciple paradigm throughout his Rule. For his part though, Benedict drops this language and rarely even alludes to the main desert themes. Since he seems uncomfortable with it, it is somewhat puzzling why he still leaves this diverting material on the anchorites in his first chapter. At any rate, a verse like this one indicates that whatever material form it takes, the monastic life is not just an institutional program but a life of personal struggle and growth toward God. And if the military language of chapter 1 seems a bit off-putting to some readers in our time, at least it symbolizes clearly enough that there is no easy way to be a monk.

August 11

If you hear this and respond "I do!" God says to you: "If you wish to have true and everlasting life, keep your tongue from evil and your lips from speaking falsely" [Ps 33(34):14]. (RB Prol. 16-17)

This part of the Prologue takes the lively form of a dialogue. Someone calls out in the marketplace: "Who desires life and longs to see good days?" A prospective "worker" calls back "I do!" It is an ideal start for a fruitful monastic life: a gracious invitation and an enthusiastic reception and response. Yet even the more mythic forms of early monastic hagiography often do not pretend that things always started out like this. Instead, we find grumpy old hermits *(Life of Pachomius)* or thoroughly ambivalent aspirants *(Life of Jerome)*. Nonetheless, it remains quite necessary to make sure no one enters the monastery *against* her own free will, or pushed into it by the vocation of another (perhaps her parent). Benedict knows well enough that people may enter monasteries for frivolous reasons, so he immediately begins to make hard demands of them. The purpose is not to drive them away but to let them know that they have undertaken a "harsh and rugged way" (RB 58.8).

August 12

The primary road to progress for the humble person is prompt obedience. (RB 5.1)

Traditional translations of this verse run: "The first step of humility is obedience without delay." Although that statement seems clear enough, it is confusing as the first, programmatic sentence of a chapter on obedience. As a matter of fact, Benedict tends to think of humility and obedience at the same time. Thus, steps two, three, and four of the ladder of humility (RB 7) have to do with obedience. Yet when we analyze them, there is at least this difference between the two virtues: humility is primarily internal, while obedience conforms to an outside authority. As such, obedience can serve as an objective antidote to the potential subjectivity of humility. Brother Joseph was the humblest monk in the entire monastery. This was shown by his fasting and his indefatigable work at menial jobs. But when he got old and sick, the abbot ordered him to take a daily siesta and to eat meat. He agreed to do so, but found it too humiliating. In this case, obedience disrupted his private world of ascetical practices. Some of the monks accused him of "holy disobedience," but others did not think it was so holy.

August 13

An hour before mealtime, the weekly servers shall each receive some bread and wine over and above the standard ration. Then they can serve the brothers at mealtime without murmuring and undue fatigue.
(RB 35.12-13)

Since the table waiters must work while the others are eating, and take their own meal after the others, Benedict grants them a preliminary snack. What is more, this is added to their usual quota. He is well aware that table waiting is hard work, especially if one hasn't eaten for twenty-four hours, as was the case on the typical monastic workday. To put off one's meal another hour could well provoke *justified* murmuring, a thing that Benedict wants to obviate. The best way to do that is by bending the rules a bit in favor of the "weak." This is a minor issue, and perhaps one that no longer applies in many monasteries, but it nevertheless serves as a window into Benedict's mentality. He recognizes that the morale of the individual is important, and it is worth seeking out little ways to maintain peace and joy in the community. It is especially worthwhile to eliminate unnecessary irritations and hardships, the kind that wear people out and get people down.

August 14

In these Lenten days, they should each accept a separate fascicle of the Bible, which they are to read straight through to the end. These books are to be given out at the beginning of Lent. (RB 48.15-16)

We have here a fascinating glimpse of the everyday life of Benedict's monks. Older translations have it that they got "books from the library," but it is quite possible that this is a reference to the various sections of the Bible itself. Ancient handwritten Bibles were very large, so they had to be bound up in sections. A whole Bible would have been enormous. The comment that they are to read them straight through is significant in that it shows there is to be no flitting about. This is serious business. But on the other hand, it could also suggest that one simply works through the Bible like any other book, thus performing *lectio divina.* I doubt very much if that is true. The old monks did not regard the biblical text as just something to be gotten through. To them, every word was precious and much of it was committed to memory. They used to walk around all day murmuring it under their breath.

August 15

But for someone who is in a rush to reach the fullness of monastic life, there are the teachings of the Holy Fathers. Anyone who carries them out will arrive at the pinnacle of perfection. (RB 73.2)

The Latin word *perfectio* turns up here (in the last chapter) for the first time in the entire Rule. In fact, it turns up *twice* (see: "fullness"). Since an epilogue should, by definition, summarize the doctrine of the main body, it is hard to see why Benedict waits this long to speak of "perfection." Actually, he seems to rely on John Cassian for much of this last chapter, and for Cassian, "perfection" is a major theme. This Latin Father, who lived a century before Benedict, was well aware that spiritual perfection for us humans can only be relative. Indeed, Cassian also knew from his acquaintance with the Desert Fathers, that the quest for perfection could also result in perfectionism, a deadly trap akin to self-salvation. But Cassian seems overly preoccupied with individual spiritual growth. We would do better to listen to Matthew 5:48, which exhorts us "Be perfect as your heavenly Father is perfect." For Matthew, the Father's perfection means all-inclusive love rather than absence of defect.

August 16

If a brother sees that any senior at all is even faintly perturbed at him or disturbed in any way, he should instantly prostrate on the floor to make satisfaction and remain there until the disturbance has been healed by a blessing. (RB 71.7)

The milk pitchers were unstable. When you filled them up, they were top heavy and the bottoms were almost rounded. In his days as a table waiter, Brother Bruno watched more than one of them tremble and teeter, but finally settle down. He knew that one day his luck would run out. Sad to say, the pitcher went over on poor, old Father Andrew, soaking his scapular from top to bottom. To make things worse, he was sitting next to the novice master, Father Nathan, who was greatly mortified. But much to Bruno's surprise, old Andrew hopped up and cheerfully shook out his scapular, spraying milk all over the refectory. It almost looked like he was having fun. When

Bruno came upstairs after lunch, Nathan was waiting for him, wringing his hands and bleating: "Go to him; ask forgiveness; beg a blessing!" So Bruno trudged down to Andrew's room and beat on the door. "Come in" said a reedy voice. "What can I do for you?" "I'm so very sorry, Father, it won't happen again." "What?" said Andrew.

August 17

If local conditions demand it or the community appeals for it reasonably and humbly, and if the prioress judges it best, then she herself, with the advice of God-fearing sisters, should choose someone and make her subprioress. (RB 65.14-15)

After many verses of grousing and grumbling, Benedict finally admits that there may be reasons to appoint a subprioress. He does not like the idea, but he will reluctantly permit it—provided the nuns ask for it in a humble, docile manner, and provided that the prioress herself appoints the subprioress she wants. What he really does not want is for her to be backed up to the wall by a "mob." Finally, he succeeds in co-opting the potential "revolt" into his system. Some scholars have suggested that this may have been precisely the kind of experience that prejudiced him so violently against the concept of a "second to the prioress." Traces of this explosion are also discernible in the last words of chapter 21, on the deans. For us today, it can be an amusing and even comforting chapter because it indicates that even for the saints of old, things did always go entirely smoothly,

August 18

The nuns should practice this zeal with the warmest love. (RB 72.3)

This seemingly banal verse could stand some unpacking. For example, the adjective "warmest" is often scaled back to "warm" by translators. Why? Do they think of Benedict as a bombastic Italian? He isn't. He is a sober old Roman, and when he uses the superlative degree, we should take him at his word. He really wants the nuns to love one another. Of course they often don't. Or rather, they don't exhibit a whole lot of affection for one another. A lot depends on temperament or culture. But we can also report that the word used here for love, namely, *amor,* is hardly a "cool" word. The New Testament avoids the Greek form of this word *(eros),* perhaps because it was too closely connected with sensuality. But Benedict shows no hesitation at all in using *amor,* especially in regard to our love for God. The combination of these two words *(ferventissimo amore)* presents the unavoidable impression that Benedict wants his community to be characterized by the fire of love more than the ice of discipline.

August 19

Let the abbot understand that he has undertaken the care of the weak, not the domination of the strong. He should fear the warning of the Prophet in which God says: "What you saw was plump you claimed for yourself, but the feeble you tossed aside" [Ezek 34.3]. (RB 27.6-7)

This verse could suggest that the monastic community is primarily therapeutic, a hospital for troubled persons. That is probably an anachronistic reading back of our preoccupations into the text. Obviously, the abbot must care for all of the monks. But where does that leave the strong? In a certain sense none of us is strong! Certainly, in a theological sense all of us are sinners and that is sometimes hard to keep in mind. Especially if we think we have put that condition behind us. But beyond that fundamental brokenness, everyone in the monastery is *infirmus*, weak, in that everyone needs guidance. It is all too easy for aggressive, confident persons to pass through a brief novitiate of humility to a lifetime of arrogant self-sufficiency. The question then becomes this: do we still have an abbot? If the abbot, in accordance with this verse, declines to "subdue" us, are we willing to remain under his care?

August 20

The eleventh step of humility is that when a sister speaks at all, she does so gently and without laughter, humbly and seriously, with few and careful words. (RB 7.60)

In Benedict's ladder of humility, steps nine, ten and eleven all deal with speech or lack thereof. But whereas step nine counsels no speech at all, this step wants "careful" *(rationabilia)* speech. From a comparison with the Rule of the Master, we know that this word replaces "holy" speech, a rather different idea. In general, the Master aims to promote a pious atmosphere, but Benedict is much more humane. He prizes civilized discourse between the sisters of the monastery as a special form of humility. It may come naturally to some persons, but others will have to work at it, and some may find it quite difficult to maintain. For historical reasons, the Trappist branch of the Benedictines banned all normal conversation for two hundred years. In the opinion of this writer, the results were heroic but misplaced. In recent years they have permitted "few and careful" words, with impressive results. Like it or not, proper speech is a necessity for all human community.

August 21

The third, and wretched, [kind of monks] are the sarabaites . . . They live in twos and threes, or even alone, without a shepherd and in their own corrals, not the Lord's. (RB 1.6, 8)

The Master and Benedict do not like the sarabaites. And why? Because they do not live under a rule and an abbot. From their sarcastic remarks, these small, informal, groups of monks are nothing but egotists who mask their narcissism by a facade of false holiness. No doubt there were such groups in the sixth century, and there probably are today as well. But we should also note an institutional bias on the part of our monastic legislators: they do not like informality. Still, it should be remembered that monastic life as such is not part of the ordinary church system, nor, indeed, of *any* system. In fact, at their best, monks and nuns can keep the church from too much resembling General Motors. In his book *O Holy Mountain!* Basil Pennington tells of visiting a hermit high up on Mount Athos. Instead of pious nostrums, the hermit shouted at the Trappist: "You western monks have got to disorganize, disorganize, disorganize!"

August 22

"Turn away from evil and do good; seek peace and pursue it"
[Ps 33(34):15]. (RB Prol. 17)

This verse is part of a dialogue in which a "worker" has eagerly answered a summons to "life and good days," probably in the form of a job. But the one in charge is not satisfied with mere enthusiasm ("I do!"). Moral demands are made. First the prospective worker is told to learn to control his tongue. Fair enough: few of us have achieved this, even in old age. But then comes a more basic requirement: "Turn away from evil and do good." Surely this goes without saying. Should someone who seeks the higher forms of spiritual existence in the monastic life need to be told to "avoid evil"? Frankly, yes. We may come to the monastery with all the best intentions, after successfully overcoming our worst faults for some time. Still, life can get long, and true evil can break through our pious facades. Further, we surely expect to find peace in the monastic life, but the psalmist and the Prologue assure us that we will need to *work* at peacemaking.

August 23

The primary road to progress for the humble person is prompt obedience.
This is characteristic of those who hold Christ more precious than
all else. (RB 5.2)

Benedict's reference to Christ as the supreme value for the monk is repeated several times in the Rule (Prol. 50; 4.10, 21; 72.12). Although monasticism is a universal cultural phenomenon, Christian monasticism is still a very specific thing. In this particular formulation, the logic seems to be that a Christian monk must be humbly obedient if he is to follow his Master, the Christ. For obedience was and is one of the central virtues of Christ himself. As the very early Christian hymn has it: "Christ became obedient for us, even to death on a cross" (see Phil 2:8). Of course, Christ's obedience was not to any earthly authority, but to his heavenly Father. Nor was his obedience limited to the Cross, but it was rather a code word for his whole way of life: "through the obedience of one, many will be made righteous" (Rom 5:19; NAB). The notion of *prompt* obedience, so much emphasized in these verses, is a carryover from the Rule of the Master and not part of the main Christian tradition.

August 24

As soon as Sunday Matins is finished, both the incoming and outgoing servers should bow before the knees of all in the oratory, asking for their prayers. (RB 35.15)

We have here a bit of monastic rubricism that some might find a bit fussy. In fact, Benedict goes on for three more verses describing this little ceremony in detail. One can still see it enacted in many monasteries. In my opinion, it is interesting because it shows that for Benedict, there was a close link between oratory and refectory. After all, these blessings could be carried out in the dining room, but they are not. They are done in church. The implication is that meals are an extension of prayers, and vice versa. For us today it is important to focus on the sacred character of the meal as such. In traditional society it was instinctively understood that what went on at table was of symbolic and religious importance. Thus one prayed before and after meals; it meant a great deal of difference who one ate with, and so on. We are well aware that dignified meals are increasingly hard to maintain in our frenetic society.

August 25

Just so, on Sunday all should be free for lectio, *except for those who are assigned to various tasks. But if someone is so negligent and slothful that he will not or cannot meditate or read, he should be assigned some work to keep him busy.* (RB 48.22-23)

Here we see Benedict the realist at his best. He wants to promote *lectio divina* on Sundays, and so he makes it a day that is not only free *from* work, but free *for lectio.* But life is not always so simple. Some jobs still have to be done around the monastery; we have no casuistry here about avoiding the least work. But beyond that, Benedict must admit that there are some people who simply cannot do *lectio.* For whatever reasons, it is impossible for them. To judge from his Rule, Pachomius would probably not admit such persons to the monastery. But Benedict is less adamant on this point. He fulminates a bit about "negligent and slothful" monks, but in the end he accommodates them. Someone who cannot bear to read is not going to have an easy time as a monk, but we should not mistake literacy for sanctity.

August 26

But for someone who is in a rush to reach the fullness of monastic life, there are the teachings of the Holy Fathers. Anyone who carries them out will arrive at the pinnacle of perfection. (RB 73.2)

The second verse of Benedict's ultimate chapter (73) is full of colorful language. "In a rush" may seem an overtranslation of *festinat*, but it is one of Benedict's favorite verbs and should not be watered down. He does not see monastic life the way my novice master did: as a sedate, dignified progression toward greater virtue. For Benedict, monastic life is a *recta via*, a straight road to heaven, and a racetrack on which one should be racing toward God (see Prol. 49). But this is not a race for flatlanders. It is a steep climb, and the peaks get higher and higher as you go. The Rule itself only leads to the lower elevations. The "pinnacle of perfection" takes something more, namely, the teachings of the Holy Fathers. If Benedict means that discipline only goes so far, his point is well taken. But if he thinks his own Rule contains no wisdom lofty enough to reach the Christian pinnacle, then he is mistaken (see RB 72).

August 27

Therefore, except for an order of the abbot or the priors appointed by him, which we permit no private command to override, all juniors must obey their seniors with every mark of loving attention. (RB 71.3-4)

It seemed like a counterintuitive move. Even though Brother Patrick was told to drive old Father Ronald to a funeral in Billings, which was to the west, now they were heading due north. Patrick did not know the territory, but he got clear instructions from the prior to just drive west on Interstate 94 until he came to Billings. But when they came to the junction of Highway 85, Ronald suddenly barked: "Turn right!" "Huh? Are you sure? I was told to go straight and make no turns" said Patrick. "And I am telling you to turn right," said Ronald, in his most authoritative voice. As they headed due north, Ronald explained that he decided to take a shortcut. What he did not tell Patrick, because he did not know it himself, was that he had forgotten where he was going in the first place. Soon the traffic thinned out and they were moving through remote badlands country, with few signs and no gas stations. The only thing that stopped them after 50 miles was a landslide, at which the state police turned them back. "Hmm," said Ronald. "We must have made a wrong turn back there somewhere."

August 28

A wise old nun should be stationed at the gate of the monastery.
She should know how to listen to people and how to speak to them . . .
As soon as someone knocks or a poor person cries out, the doorkeeper
should answer "Thanks be to God!" or "Please bless me!" (RB 66.1, 3)

The receptionist of the monastery plays an important role. She is not a mere functionary but rather the face, as it were, of the community toward the world. Often when visitors come to the monastery they are in need, so it is very important that they not be discouraged by a harsh response. Notice that Benedict is concerned that the gatekeeper know how to listen and how to speak. Probably Benedict even expected his portress to be able to give spiritual direction. Why does he tell her to cry out "Thanks be to God" or "Please bless me!"? Isn't it the visitor who should be saying such things? Who is the needy one? Apparently, the portress thinks that the visitor is an almost divine gift to the monastery. At least that is the theology of the chapter on hospitality (RB 53) and it is repeated here.

August 29

"Each person is endowed by God with a particular gift, some for this, some for that" (1 Cor 7:7). Therefore it is with some hesitation that we set down rules for others in the matter of consumption. (RB 40.1-2)

Here we have a monastic founder, indeed *the* greatest monastic founder, expressing hesitation about running other peoples' lives! A cursory knowledge of monastic history shows that by no means have all of Benedict's followers possessed his sensitivity to the rights of others. He grounds his approach in Scripture, which teaches that God gives different persons different gifts. Therefore, anyone who tries to force them all onto one procrustean bed will be guilty of disrespect toward the Creator as well as the persons. It should be noted, however, that just because Benedict hesitates to use his authority to impose sumptuary legislation on his monks, this does not exempt the individual monk from personal discipline. Just as I am the best judge of my own capacity for food and drink, I must shoulder the responsibility of living within my own limits. I cannot blame an indulgent abbot for my own lack of discipline.

August 30

Let the abbot imitate the loving example of the Good Shepherd: he left ninety-nine sheep in the hills to go looking for one sheep that had gone astray. He was so filled by sympathy at its weakness that "he mercifully placed it on his" sacred "shoulders" and carried it back to the flock [Luke 15:5]. (RB 27.8-9)

St. Luke's parable has often struck people, especially those of a rural background, as wildly unrealistic. It is helpful to know that the parables were written with the purpose of shocking us into a new level of insight about the Kingdom of God. But the first lesson is that God's ways are not our ways. What looks like imprudence to us is just another example of God's prodigal, extravagant love for each one of us. In order to make this point in regard to the abbot, Benedict has even "retouched" Luke's parable to make it more evocative. He has succeeded in creating an extremely poignant vignette that is hard to forget. But how is an abbot to put this kind of idealism into everyday practice? When does consideration for a troubled member become *de facto* neglect of the community?

August 31

The twelfth step of humility comes about when a monk's humility is not only in his heart, but is apparent in his very body to those who see him. (RB 7.62)

In this twelfth step, the Master and Benedict apparently attempt to balance off John Cassian's emphasis on the internalization of the virtue of humility. To do this, they put a great emphasis on the physical signs of the humble person. Since this is the final step of the ladder of humility, it might seem that the physical is being glorified at the expense of the spiritual. But we need not take it quite that way; perhaps better to say that true humility should pervade the whole of the person, which includes the body. Rightly taken, there is something deeply Christian about this emphasis, for the Incarnation of God in Jesus Christ had precisely the same intent: to effect the divinization of the whole person, soul and body. Furthermore, we say that we believe in the resurrection of the body and not just the soul (immortality). So the spirituality promoted by Benedict is not ethereal, but quite down to earth. This is not to negate Cassian's point that one must internalize this piety.

September 1

The fourth kind of monks are called gyrovagues . . . They are ever on the move and never stable. (RB 1.10-11)

The complaint against the gyrovagues is that they are hedonists and gluttons. They refuse to buckle down to a committed monastic life in one place but are always in search of a better meal, a better wine. This critique of wandering monks is developed into a huge satire by the Master, but reduced by Benedict to a few choice words. Probably at the root of it is the ancient monastic conviction that the only way to make any spiritual progress is to stop running around; one must finally confront oneself. As an ancient monastic proverb has it, "Your cell will teach you everything." Nevertheless, monks had to travel a lot on business (see RB 67). And some very fine Irish monks deliberately took up wandering as a means of doing penance. In their view, to leave Ireland was the acutest form of suffering. One does not have to be blind to a certain restlessness in them to still appreciate their sincerity. What is more, without them the Christianization of Frankish Europe would have been a lot more difficult.

September 2

When you have done this, my eyes will gaze on you and my ears will hear your prayers; and before you even call on me, I will say to you: "Here I am!" [Isa 58:9; 65:24]. (RB Prol. 18)

According to the words from Isaiah, God will look on us and hear us only after we have done "this," namely, done good and avoided evil. As it stands, that is perfectly good merit theology, but it does not go nearly far enough. Following Isaiah 65:24, the Prologue also claims that God will respond to us even before we call on him. This verse then provides a salutary corrective to the *quid pro quo* arrangement that is often presented as Christian ethics. For the truth is that we could not even call on God if he had not first "gazed" on us and "heard" us. The idea of God forever looking at us and hearing us may seem oppressive, and even a denial of our freedom. But the alternative, the idea that we are truly "on our own" in the universe, is much heavier for most of us to bear. To know that God is accompanying us every step of the way should be a great support and comfort.

September 3

As soon as something is commanded by the superior, they waste no time in executing it as if it were divinely commanded. (RB 5.4)

This verse, and several that follow it, on the need for alacrity in monastic obedience, could have an ominous ring to it. In the experience of most people, instant obedience is proper to dogs and military boot camp, not free and mature adults. It is the hallmark of tyranny to demand instantaneous, unquestioning obedience to all its commands, so it seems out of place in a religious document. In answer to these feelings of uneasiness, at least two points might be made: (1) Benedict bases the authority of his abbot on the very authority of God, but he does not confuse the two things. "As if" allows for a bit of slippage, at least enough to remind both abbot and subject that the abbot, too, is a sinner and not always a pure conduit for the will of God. (2) In the code language of the sixth century, alacrity could stand for wholeheartedness. That is to say that one can express his *eagerness* to obey by his *haste* in doing so.

September 4

We read that wine is absolutely not for monks. But since monks in our day cannot be convinced of this, let us at least agree not to drink to excess, but sparingly. " For wine makes even the wise go astray" [Sir 19:2]. (RB 40.6-7)

New Year's Eve was not a fun time in the novitiate. As if to emphasize their departure from "the world," the novices were given nothing special for recreation. They were playing their usual game of *mah jong* when the door burst open with a surprise: Father George bearing a tray of double martinis! Of course, the novice master did not know, and he could appear any second, so Novice Timothy grabbed a drink and downed it in one gulp. Wasn't he surprised when his chest and shoulders began to tighten, and he could hardly breathe. What was wrong? What to do? He could not go in and lie down; they were forbidden to do that. He could not tell the novice master what he had done. He went outside in ten below and walked in circles. In his mind was a possible headline: "Local monk dies of alcohol poisoning on New Year's Eve."

September 5

The life of a monk should have a Lenten quality about it at all times. But since few have that much strength, we urge them during these days of Lent to preserve the purity of their lives. (RB 49.1-2)

This first sentence of the chapter on Lent is quintessential Benedict. He first invokes the heroic, and mostly mythic, monastic tradition and then he adds ruefully that we lesser beings of the present day will probably find it too demanding. If we cannot meet *the* standard, well, let us at least meet *a* standard. Interesting, and even amusing, as this is to think about, it is not necessarily true. The church herself has never proposed that her members practice constant penance; we have both fasts and feasts. As for the monks, they may set out to avoid all festivity, but they usually learn that it is psychologically necessary to include it in their lives. The greatest danger is excess, and a plunge into exactly the opposite of what one claims to want. Those churches which had the greatest disdain for the Catholic practice of a mere forty days of penance had a sorry tendency to end with *no* Lent themselves.

September 6

"That the Whole Fulfillment of Justice Is Not Laid Down in This Rule"
(RB 73, title)

The title of Benedict's epilogue (last chapter) is, to say the least, intriguing. On first glance, it appears to be merely one expression of a point that will be made several more times in main body of chapter 73, namely, that the Holy Rule should not be thought to be the fullness of monastic wisdom. But one wonders if something more doesn't lurk in this puzzling title. It looks very much like Jesus' insistence in Matthew 3:15 that John the Baptist baptize him "so that all justice might be fulfilled." If Benedict is thinking of Matthew's Gospel, which is his favorite, he may well have been aware that "justice" for that evangelist is no mere matter of legal or moral rights. Rather, it encompasses the whole of Christian righteousness, which means the fullness of spiritual life in God. Perhaps Benedict just means that one does not reach this level by merely obeying monastic rules. They are just the framework within which one may find it easier to live a life of union with God. And it could well be that Benedict himself did not concoct this title.

September 7

The Office of Vespers should be arranged so that they need not eat by lamplight. Everything should be completed by the light of day.
(RB 41.8)

This verse reminds us what life was like before the advent of modern technology. People had to conform their activities to the rhythms of nature, even if it meant eating at times that were not ideal. Of course, with the monks there was also the issue of frugality. Lamps cost money, especially if the community was large enough to need many of them. But most likely Benedict is more concerned that the horarium bend to the contours of nature. There is a certain humility about living according to the local circumstances, even when one has an alternative. For a century now, the industrial West has substituted an artificial lifestyle for a natural one. We can do it because of the invention of electricity and so on. We can turn night into day, and vice versa. But we should not forget that we do so at a price. And the day may come when we simply have to learn to live more simply.

September 8

Filled with the gentleness that comes from the fear of God, the portress should quickly respond with the warmest charity. If she needs help, she should be given a younger sister to help her. (RB 66.4-5)

"The gentleness that comes from the fear of God" is a memorable expression. How does the fear of God produce gentleness? Perhaps the specific context has something to do with that. Visitors are to be treated gently because Christ is seen in them. To put it in biblical terms, God is feared in them. This requires that the monastic portress approach her job differently than the typical doorkeeper. Often, the secular doorkeeper sees her job as primarily to keep people out, to guard a precious enclosure from contamination by the world. That is not the monastic mentality. The monastic community exists for no other reason than to witness to God's love for the world. And clearly the portress must exemplify that theological truth in a special way. Superiors should be particularly wary of leaving a gruff old troll in the portress' office, as seems to happen too often in monasteries.

September 9

The use of baths should be offered to the sick as often as it is useful, but less readily to the healthy and especially to the young. (RB 36.8)

What could be the use of restricting persons' bathing practices? In the very next verse, Benedict also restricts the eating of meat by all but the sick. In both cases, the underlying motive was probably ascetical: warm water and heat-causing food could stimulate sexual drives. Today we would probably scoff at such attitudes, although legions of people now avoid red meat for equally exotic reasons. As for bathing, most Americans today wash far, far more than they did fifty years ago. So these are variable matters of culture, not principle. Still, it is quite true that people should not extend the privileges of the sick to all of life. It is quite tempting for some personalities to fall into a pattern of self-indulgence; a critical mass of such attitudes can leave us with a therapeutic institution rather than a monastery. By and large, a monastery without discipline is an anomaly.

September 10

If a brother has been punished often for some fault but does not change even after excommunication, a harsher penalty should be applied to him: he should be beaten with rods. (RB 28.1)

Benedict lived in an age where corporal punishment was routine. For example, inmates of Bedlam, the London insane asylum, were simply beaten with rods. On occasion, that included King George III! Probably they had no idea what else to do with them. Even though it is as violent as any age in history, our society generally forbids corporal punishment. What then do we do with incorrigibles? That is what Benedict is discussing here: people who will not mend their ways. He has already tried other means, especially excommunication, but they have not worked. In our own day and age, it would seem that the problem is not excessive punishment but rather *neglect*. In other words, we simply abandon troubled people, perhaps because we do not love them enough to engage personally in their healing.

September 11

Whether [the monk] is at the Divine Office, in the oratory, in the monastery, in the garden, on a journey, in the field or anywhere at all, whether sitting, walking or standing, let his head be bowed and his eyes be directed downward. (RB 7.63)

This extraordinary verse functions as the twelfth step of humility. It is copied from the Rule of the Master, who is prone to carry things too far and to make his points with a heavy hand. There is something almost crassly materialistic about this verse, but after all the point of step twelve is to insist on physical humility. The verse goes on to dictate the proper posture for a humble monk: head bowed and eyes downcast. In traditional Benedictine language, this was *custodia oculorum*, the guarding of the eyes. Some literalistic novice masters actually had their charges move around the monastery in this fashion: hands under the scapular, head bowed and eyes downcast. In fact, a few monks took on this pose in their lifelong self-presentation. There was nothing wrong with that in itself. It is probably better than a strutting or preening. But one should not judge people from their posture.

September 12

So let us with God's help set out to arrange things for that most vigorous type of monk, the cenobite. (RB 1.13)

The descriptive adjective that Benedict uses for the cenobite is *fortissimum*, "most vigorous." Unfortunately, we are not sure what he means. The word *fortis* can mean many things. Possibly it refers to the fact that the cenobites "fight together." But a more interesting interpretation could come from the Life of Pachomius (SBo 105). When he was asked whether the anchorites are superior to the cenobites, he told a parable that made his point gently but firmly. He said that in his opinion the cenobites are more admirable. Why? Because the anchorite is like a merchant who sells very ordinary commodities. By living apart, he takes very little chance—but he also makes little profit. But the cenobite lives a much riskier life in the midst of people, where there is ample opportunity for both good and evil in human interactions. Hence, the cenobite is playing for much higher stakes and for that reason should receive a higher reward. Perhaps that is the meaning of "most vigorous"?

September 13

Dearest brothers, what could be sweeter to our ears than this voice of the Lord that invites us? (RB Prol. 19)

At this point, the preacher addresses a whole group of hearers, presumably monks. In fact, the Prologue switches from the singular to the plural already in verse 5. For practical purposes, the whole Prologue can be taken as an exhortation to a whole community, and probably a group of veteran monks. The preacher, surely the abbot, does not consider them a faceless crowd; they are his "dearest brothers." In couching his message in such warmly personal terms, the author makes his own the spirit of the Prologue, which presents God in very personal terms. It does not just quote the Bible as a neutral document. It takes the biblical teaching as the living voice of the Lord. And even though the message is sometimes harsh and demanding, it is basically a loving invitation to us from God. There may be threats, but the overall thrust of the Prologue is to urge us to come to God. As such, it ought to be "sweet to our ears." What could be more encouraging and consoling than this invitation?

September 14

"Whoever listens to you listens to me." [Luke 10:16] (RB 5.6, 15)

In order to provide a solid biblical foundation for his doctrine of quick and willing obedience in chapter 5, Benedict quotes Luke 10:16 not once, but two times. This verse, in which Jesus designates his disciples as his full, accredited representatives, is applied here to abbot and monk: whoever listens to the abbot listens to Jesus Christ. The breathtaking simplicity of this claim does not mitigate its radicality. The very idea that one human being can infallibly find the will of God mediated through another human being is something that even the New Testament does not lightly claim. And in fact it can be a formula for disaster unless the following caveats are in place: (1) Although the abbot receives this mandate because of his office and not because of his personal endowment, nevertheless, this does not excuse him from the task of prayerfully seeking the will of God. (2) The Christian disciple is never excused from exercising the discernment of conscience toward a given demand of authority.

September 15

The sick should remember that they are being served out of respect for God. So they should not annoy the brothers serving them with trivial demands. Still, they should be patiently borne with, for by such things we merit a generous reward. (RB 36.4-5)

After enunciating the lofty demands of Matthew 25 regarding care of the sick, Benedict attempts to work out some of the possible problems that might arise. Following Basil, (Latin Rule 36), Benedict warns the sick not to take advantage of their special position. But it should be pointed out that this is an addition to Jesus' teaching in Matthew; he does not say we should serve the *deserving* sick, he says we should serve the sick as they are. It is true that sometimes the sick need to be admonished to behave themselves, but their obnoxious behavior may be part of their sickness. In the end, Benedict recognizes that care of the sick demands patience, which is one of his favorite virtues. At the close of the Prologue he does not hesitate to say that patience associates us with the suffering of Christ himself, and that it will lead us to eternal life with him.

September 16

In these days [of Lent] each one, of his own will with the joy of the Holy Spirit, can offer God something beyond what is imposed on him. (RB 49.6)

Even though Benedict wants the whole community to follow a set pattern of Lenten penance, he also urges the individual monk to decide what he alone will carry out. Monks are not mere robots or cogs in a machine, fit to carry out only what has been imposed from above. They also need to decide what they as individuals need to do *this* Lent. This is an exercise of the will, which is a thing that some monastic commentators seem to find abhorrent in a monk. Not at all! Without the full engagement of the individual will, there really is no spirituality. But the thing is not just a grim exercise in will power either. It is to be done "with the joy of the Holy Spirit." Not out of obligation, not even out of obedience, but out of pure joy. Benedict rarely mentions the Spirit, but when he does, it is with maximum effect.

September 17

We have sketched out this Rule so that by carrying it out in monasteries we may show that we at least have moral decency and the rudiments of monastic life. (RB 73.1)

Here is the beginning of Benedict's epilogue, chapter 73. It is a rather awkward and pedantic statement, but the sentiments are not at all pompous. In what almost looks like a disclaimer, the author insists that his Rule is not the last word. He has merely "sketched out" *(descripsimus)* a Rule, which he will later call "modest" (v. 8). And even if we carry out this little Rule to the letter, it will be no high standard, just "moral decency" and "the rudiments of monastic life." Anyone who has tried to live up to the demands of the Rule might wince at this disclaimer, and we might be tempted to set it aside as an expression of false modesty by the author. It is hard to know just what to make of this statement, but it cannot change what the Rule really is, namely, a monastic expression of the Gospel itself. And the previous chapter (72), with its lofty demands for love, is no "little Rule" but an exquisite distillation of the ethics of Jesus.

September 18

The brothers, however, should offer their advice with all deference and humility, not presuming to assert their views in a bold manner. (RB 3.4)

The subject of alms was a bone of contention on the senior council. Abbot Raymond often asked for advice about this or that request, but there seemed to be no consistency in his approach. Sometimes he wondered what do about a request for five thousand dollars, and sometimes it was five dollars that bothered him. What was obvious to everyone was that he did not want to give any alms at all, since he thought that monasteries should receive them, not disperse them. He typically ended these discussions with the dictum: "We need a policy!" One day Father Gilbert had enough, so he offered to research the matter and come back with a policy. Abbot Raymond agreed, but he was secretly vexed. In fact, the last thing he wanted was a policy. As for Gilbert, he had a hard time finding out what other monasteries were doing. He had to conclude that *none* of them had a policy. Nevertheless, he put together a simple proposal and gave it to the abbot. He was surely surprised, then, when the abbot brought *two* proposals to the council for discussion: Gilbert's and his own. "Sorry," said Gil, "we can only discuss one policy at a time. Take your pick, yours or mine." "Oh alright, we'll take yours" muttered the abbot.

September 19

If possible, the monastery should be situated with all necessities such as water, mill and garden contained within the walls so the various crafts can be practiced there. Then it will not be necessary for the nuns to move about outside, which is certainly not good for their souls.
(RB 66.6-7)

The sixth century was a turbulent one, so turbulent that to take to the Italian roads was to take one's life in one's hands. Monks and nuns needed to be protected from marauding bands of Lombards and Ostrogoths. And often the walls were not enough. Monte Cassino (Benedict's monastery) was sacked about 577, twenty-five years after the saint's death. But external dangers were not the only problem. The nuns themselves could become worldly by merely spending too much time outside the cloister. So Benedict tries to create a self-sufficient environment for them. In the early medieval period such a project was relatively practical. Nowadays it is less so. We can build all the walls we want; if the mass media is given free access, the world is with us. "Flight from the world" is largely a matter of mind, not walls.

September 20

The sick sisters should be given . . . an attendant who is God-fearing, devoted and careful. (RB 36.7)

The Latin term that is here translated as "attendant" is in fact *servitor* (server). We might wonder why Benedict did not use the more intelligible word "nurse," but that is mostly a modern term. Even though "server" seems colorless and generic, it has the great advantage of echoing an immensely important biblical theme, namely, the Servant of YHWH. In the last of his four Servant Songs (53.10), the prophet Isaiah says that this servant will give his life for the rescue of the people by the abolition of their sins. Seven centuries later, the Christians found this a helpful way of thinking about Jesus' death on the cross. By calling the monastic nurse *servitor,* therefore, Benedict could be associating her with the self-sacrifice of Christ. A few verses earlier, Benedict tells us that when we *serve* the sick (36.1), we serve Christ himself. So it could be claimed that we have here a complete circle of devotion to Christ: to serve Christ as Christ himself would do.

September 21

If [the troubled monk] still does not improve, or if, God forbid! he even gets carried away by pride and tries to defend his actions, then the abbot should proceed like a skilled physician. (RB 28.2-3)

In explanation of these verses, Benedict proceeds to discuss various methods of correction with medical imagery: hot packs, oil, medicine, cautery. It is sometimes suggested that Benedict was himself skilled in medical arts, but that seems unlikely. In those days, everyone knew a little medicine. More important here is the general image of the abbot as physician. Certainly this is based upon the saying of Jesus given in Matthew 9:12: "Those who are well do not need a physician, but the sick do." The point would seem to be that whatever else the abbot finds he must do—fund raising, teaching, building—his primary responsibility is to the spiritual well-being of his brothers. And if they are troubled, then he may have to employ methods that are painful at the time but ultimately therapeutic. To decline to do so is a confused form of cruelty. Like the dentist who hesitates to drill deep enough, such neglect of duty simply defers problems to another day and probably worsens them.

September 22

Always aware of his guilt for sins, he should consider himself to be already standing before the terrifying judgment. (RB 7.64)

Found as it is in the twelfth step of humility, this verse is a bit puzzling. A few lines later Benedict will tell us that his ladder of humility has climbed from fear to love. But surely this verse is less about love than it is about fear. What is going on here? In a very important sense, true religion *never* leaves fear behind. If by fear we mean a healthy awareness that we are sinners and will always remain sinners, then it is not to be transcended. Of course, it is not so pleasant to hear about my sins and the impending judgment, but the New Testament never hides this reality from the Christian disciple. An unwillingness or perhaps an inability to accept this state of affairs constitutes a basic lack of Christian humility that goes beyond anything discussed in the other steps of the ladder of humility. Having said that, it must be admitted that many modern people find a formulation such as this to be rather crushing. One must remember that love is the point.

September 23

[The abbot] is believed to represent Christ in the monastery, since he is called by his name. (RB 2.2)

According to Benedict, the abbot is called *abba*, just as Christ is. This might surprise us, since it is well known that *abba* means "father" in biblical parlance, and in fact Christ often addresses his "Father in heaven" as *Abba*. How then is Christ *abba*? According to the church fathers, he is our father in the realm of grace. Basil (Latin Rule 4) says that anyone who has begotten another through the Gospel should be called father. According to this logic, Christ is indeed our Father. But the important corollary here is that it is also the abbot's role to "beget others through the Gospel." He may have to play many roles—counselor, administrator, teacher—but he should remember that all of them point to one end: to engender children for the kingdom of God. When he says that the abbot "represents" Christ the father, he avoids saying that he (the abbot) *is* the father of the monks. Nor is his role to make disciples for himself. His is strictly a role of agency: Christ acts through him in the monastery.

September 24

Therefore, let us put on, like a belt around our waist, the faith that leads to the performance of good works. (RB Prol. 21)

Because the style of clothing of most modern readers of the Rule is quite different from that of the ancients, we may miss the significance of this verse. A voluminous, flowing robe was comfortable and practical for ordinary wear in a warm climate, but too bulky for strenuous physical activity. Therefore, it had to be gathered at the waist to allow free movement. In the present application, "faith" is compared to the belt that prepares us for vigorous action or "good works." This is a summary of the whole Prologue, which demands practical implementation of the call and invitation of God. In biblical parlance, the girding of loins was usually a preparation for the voice of God and of carrying out his commands. Like the people of the Exodus, we should have our "loins girt, sandals on our feet, staff in hand" (see Exod 12:11; NAB). Luke 12:35 gives it an eschatological connotation: "Let your loins be girded and your lamps burning, and be like servants waiting for their master to come home from the wedding feast" (RSV).

September 25

Command and response occur almost simultaneously with an alacrity caused by the fear of the Lord. It is love that drives these people to progress toward eternal life. (RB 5.9)

In this verse, certain ideas are juxtaposed in a way that could cause confusion or even scandal. The mention of "fear" in the same sentence with "instant obedience" sets up a very worrisome dynamic that is typical of life in a dysfunctional society. Found in a Christian, monastic rule like Benedict's, such ideas seem to have no place. But closer reading shows that the fear in question here is actually "fear of the Lord," a biblical value that is by no means synonymous with abject terror. This is shown by the mention of "love" in the very next line: fear of the Lord and love are very close in the mind of the early Christian thinkers. It is also clear that for Benedict, the only proper motivation for prompt obedience is love. Anything else suggests a slavishness and a subordination that is demeaning to the human person. Monastic life is meant to build people up, not to crush them.

September 26

In community, prayer should be very brief indeed, and when the superior gives the sign, all should rise up together. (RB 20.5)

It is sometimes said that Benedict is against long, drawn-out prayers. That may be true, but it is not what this verse is about. "Prayer" here probably refers to the silent prostrations that the old monks sometimes made *between* the psalms in the Divine Office. These are sometimes called "psalm prayers." Since everything must be done in unison in public prayer, these prayers also must be done together. Coming after some verses calling for "pure" prayer, this verse reminds us of a point that Cassian makes over and over about the brevity of "pure" prayer. For him, such prayer only flares up for a moment in the midst of "prayers" such as the psalms. It was said of one of the Pachomian monks that he used to sit in his cell plaiting ropes and murmuring the psalms. Periodically prayer would well up in his heart, whereupon he would prostrate for a brief time. Of course, it is a somewhat different situation when we make such "prayer" together.

September 27

The monk should deny his body some food, some drink, some chatter, some joking, and let him await holy Easter with joyful spiritual desire.
(RB 49.7)

Does Benedict wish to outlaw humor in his monastery? If so, he is risking psychological ruin. But look again. He is not asking for long faces, but a little less frivolity. That implies that joking and banter were a regular feature of community life. Perhaps not for everybody; they are not everybody's cup of tea. But you don't ask people to cut back from what is already forbidden! The main thrust of this verse, however, is the magnificent advice to "await holy Easter with joyful spiritual desire." That means that the real purpose of Lent is not to eradicate desire, but to intensify it. This verse assumes that one heightens desire for God by banking the other little fires in one's life. How can we sharpen our longing for God? We probably cannot do this by some kind of unwise exclusion of all other desires from our lives. Taken in moderate degree, they are not opposed to God. Properly used, they can enhance our love for him.

September 28

May Christ lead us altogether to life everlasting. (RB 72.12)

This is the great final prayer of Benedict's Holy Rule, so it is of exceptional importance for understanding his spirit. As with many of the verses of this last chapter, this one has a crucially important adverb: "altogether." Someone consulting an older translation of the Rule might be surprised to find the word rendered as "likewise," or possibly not rendered at all. How could that be? The Latin word, *pariter,* is rather unusual, and it is capable of either a weak or strong interpretation. Probably because of their predispositions, earlier commentators missed the radical communal implications of this word. If we take it in its strongest, literal, sense, it means that Christ will lead the whole community to heaven! Christian catechesis has often portrayed heavenly life in rather individualistic terms: "Me 'n' Jesus." But in this great eschatological prayer, we Benedictines pray that we may continue forever to live as we have been living: together. If we are just "putting up with each other," this prayer can be quite disconcerting. But if we are striving to love each other as members of Christ, it can be a great consolation.

September 29

It is the abbot's responsibility to signal the time for the work of God, both during the day and the night. He should either give the signal himself or entrust the work to a careful brother. That way, everything will be done at the right time. (RB 57.1)

In most monasteries the novices ring the bells, and Incarnation Abbey was no exception. In fact, the novice master used to warn his charges that anyone who neglected this duty could expect to find himself on the next train home. No wonder, then, that during his first week as bell ringer, Novice Walbert was a nervous wreck. He set two alarm clocks, but he still could not be sure he would not sleep right through them at 4:15 a.m. when he had to rise. Consequently, he had a hard time getting to sleep, and he tended to wake up every hour or so to make sure the clocks had not stopped. Finally his worst fears were realized: he overslept! Or at least that's what he had to conclude from the sound of many footsteps tramping the wooden hallway floors. Walbert jumped out of bed and rushed to the bell rope in his pajamas, wildly ringing the bell for all he was worth. But it turned out that the monks were just coming in from a basketball game at 10:30 p.m.

September 30

No one should dare to tell anyone else what she has seen or heard outside the monastery, a thing that causes much harm. (RB 67.5)

Although Benedict knows it will be necessary to send the nuns on business journeys, he does not want them to talk about what they have seen. Apparently, he is worried about scandalous and titillating things that could prove to be a stumbling block for those who stay home. He is struggling to keep the world from invading the monastery. But he seems to take no account of those aspects of the world that are important for nuns and monks to know. For example, we need to know about the sufferings of people who are being crushed by war, starvation and so forth. There is no virtue at all in naive ignorance. Such ignorance is not bliss; it is a shame. This information is available in the mass media, and monasteries must decide how much of that commodity they will allow into their midst. But there is a real danger that some religious develop a sort of addiction to the news, which often seems to anesthetize people from doing anything constructive.

October 1

Although human nature itself is inclined to be indulgent to these two age-groups, namely, the aged and children, the authority of the Rule should also look out for them. (RB 37.1)

In his tiny chapter 37 Benedict arranges for early snacks for the very old and the children, since they would find it burdensome to wait for a single, daily meal at mid-afternoon or sunset. More notable, though, is his introductory dictum about general human tenderness toward these two age groups. One wonders whether this cheerful remark is based on actual observation or whether it is simply a rhetorical ploy on the part of the author? For the fact is that people are *not* always kind toward the aged and the little ones. Indeed, sometimes they are savage toward them and when that happens the law must step in to protect them. The Jewish Bible always makes it clear that the good king is one who shelters the "widow and the orphan." In any age, a government that does not carry out this sacred duty does not deserve the allegiance of its people. Unfortunately, we see numerous examples of this in modern times. Benedict simply will not allow this to happen in his monastery.

October 2

But if even [various punishments] do not heal him, then the time has come for the abbot to wield the knife of amputation . . . the danger is that one sick sheep might infect the whole flock. (RB 28.7-8)

On rare occasions, it may be necessary for an abbot to expel one of the members from the community. The church is very concerned about the rights of the individual, so a careful canonical procedure must be followed. But there is general acknowledgement that some persons must be sent away for the good of the community. Perhaps we should say for the *salvation* of the community, for we are only talking here about cases in which the gravest harm is being done. A social organism that cannot defend itself from a toxic member is in serious danger of dissolution. The origins of the problem may be a lack of standards for entry, a thing that is by no means unknown in modern monasteries. But in addition, healthy and holy monks have the same possibility as anyone else to choose the bad and themselves become bad. When this happens they are no longer in the right place and must be helped to find a more appropriate one.

October 3

When he has climbed all these steps of humility, the monk will soon arrive at that "perfect love of God that drives out fear" [1 John 4:18]. (RB 7.67)

Benedict's use of this text from the First Letter of John seems perfect for his purposes, for it claims that the ladder of humility culminates in love. No one can deny that the end of all true religion is love; and it is also undeniable that fear has its drawbacks. However, it might be added that this formulation begs questions like "what kind of fear?" and "what kind of love?" First John says "perfect" love drives out fear. The great Johannine commentator Raymond E. Brown claimed that "perfect" love does not mean love without defects, but rather the love of God that finds itself incarnated in human beings. What is more, there is a basic religious fear (which might be given another name like "awe") that ought not to be left behind. Love without this kind of fear can be mere maudlin sentiment or worse. To put it another way, each of the steps of humility is also a particular manifestation of love—and fear. When the two things are kept apart, then starts trouble.

October 4

For the Apostle says: You have received the Spirit of adoption of sons, which makes us cry out: "Abba, Father!" [Rom 8:15]. (RB 2.3)

The word Spirit is capitalized here to make a point. In the Pauline original it is lower case, as a contrast to "spirit of slavery." But since the Rule mentions the Holy Spirit so seldom, we use it here to emphasize that the third person of the Trinity is not entirely absent from the document. After all, if we are to acknowledge the abbot as the representative of Christ, we must have faith. Apart from this, there is no particular reason to put the abbot on such a pedestal. But where does faith really come from? It comes from the presence of the Holy Spirit in our hearts. Of course, the point in Romans is that adoptive filiation causes every Christian to cry "*Abba*, Father." And that cry is addressed to the Father in heaven. To transfer that kind of ecstatic faith to a human representative of God/Christ is a difficult business, but it lies close to the heart of cenobitic monasticism.

October 5

Let us set out on his path with the Gospel as our guide, so that we may be worthy to see him who has called us into his kingdom. (RB Prol. 21)

The idea of the "Gospel as our guide" is repeated in RB 73.3: "What page, what passage of the inspired books of the Old and New Testaments is not the truest of guides for human life?" When an idea is repeated at the beginning and end of an ancient document (an "inclusion"), a special emphasis is meant. The Bible is only a guide for those who read it regularly and consciously make it their guide for life. The Prologue uses the term "Gospel" in place of "Bible" in this verse, and it is true that the New Testament is a more precise guide than the Old Testament for the Christian. Yet it is doubtful if the author was conscious of any dichotomy. For the early Christians, the entire Bible was the voice of Christ. Consequently, there is nothing surprising about the fact that the Prologue mainly employs the Old Testament psalms to make its point.

October 6

They do not wish to run their own lives, obeying their own desires and wants. Rather, they prefer to walk according to the judgment and command of another, living in cenobitic community with an abbot over them. (RB 5.12)

The whole idea of voluntarily submitting one's entire life to the "judgment of another" strikes many people in our society as preposterous, if not downright pathological. Why would someone voluntarily forego basic choices in favor of following the plans of someone else? Does this not run contrary to the very essence of modern freedom? There are those for whom personal decision and responsibility become too much, so they look for someone else to "run their lives." Anyone who manifests these tendencies should be firmly excluded from the cenobitic community. But it is quite possible to set aside basic personal freedom in exchange for spiritual leadership that helps one to transcend mere self-interest. Understood in the right way, submission to an abbot can free me from the internal shackles that block the way to true freedom. When I no longer have to plan every aspect of my life, I am much freer to spend myself without counting the cost.

October 7

"What if my thoughts are not humble? What if I rise up in pride?
Then you will refuse me as a mother does a weaned child"
(Ps 130[131]:2). (RB 7.4)

The Master and Benedict make effective use of Psalm 130(131) to prove their ascetic teaching that pride is spiritually destructive. But to do so, they have to turn things around a bit, and even contradict the psalm. Far from the negative idea of a weaned child being rejected, the psalm really says that the weaned child is content to merely cling to the mother. Already with the Old Latin translation of the Hebrew Bible, this image got inverted to claim that the weaned child is rejected by the mother. Actually, the original sense would have served the monastic authors better than the one they found in their Latin Bible! The weaned child could symbolize the humble person who no longer makes any insistent demands on God or anyone else. This is one case, and there are many in the monastic Rules, where the authors do not completely understand the sacred text. But they nevertheless manage to make it come out all right.

October 8

But each sister should tell prioress what she wishes to do [during Lent], so it will be done with her blessing and approval. For whatever is done without the permission of the spiritual mother will be counted as presumption and vainglory, not deserving a reward. (RB 49.8-9)

During Lent, Benedict wants the community to develop a common set of penitential practices for its members. But he also urges the individuals to go beyond the common norms by adding some personal dimension to their practice. That is a remarkable turn toward the individual by a very communitarian thinker. Nevertheless, he still finds it necessary to hedge in this concession with the demand that it be done with abbatial approval. Some modern monasteries ask their members to present the prioress with a brief list of their *bona opera* (good works) at the beginning of Lent. Before giving her blessing, the superior may ask that the list be modified. To our modern eyes, that may seem an irritating intrusion into the freedom of the individual. But this transaction can provide the individual with some authoritative outside "feedback" before embarking on her Lenten journey.

October 9

They should prefer absolutely nothing to Christ. (RB 72.11)

This famous dictum of Benedict appears here for the second time. In chapter 4 (v. 21), he says virtually the same thing, but probably it means more to him at the end of the Rule. A lifetime of faithfulness must have deepened his understanding of exactly how much such a principle actually costs. It is also helpful to know that the quote comes originally from St. Cyprian's commentary on the Our Father: "We should prefer nothing to Christ, for he preferred nothing to us" (*LP* 15). The christological reference here is not generic or vague; it means that he suffered and died for our sins on the cross. Also that he rose on our behalf on the third day. To know the full quote helps keep all this in perspective, for we ought not place too much importance on *our* preference for Christ. At any rate this mention of Christ as the object of our whole life as monastics is very timely, since this is really the final statement of the entire Rule. Chapter 73 is an epilogue, not the true finale.

October 10

When they rise for the Work of God, they should gently encourage each other to offset the excuses of the drowsy. (RB 22.8)

In addition to ringing the bells, the novices were expected to rouse each monk individually. This task involved a knock on the door, with the greeting, *"Benedicite!"* The inhabitant was expected to answer *"Deus!"* As it stood, the exchange made no grammatical sense, but it worked well enough for monks who had no difficulty getting out of bed. However, those who were not in that category sometimes threw shoes and even less savory objects at the door. None of this was personal. One week when he was bell ringer, Frater (clerical novice) Aelred set his alarm wrong and he got up in the middle of the night knocking on doors. Since it was one o'clock in the morning, it was no surprise that no one answered his greeting, but he did not catch on. Finally he got to the door of Abbot Eugene. Here, he got a response. The Abbot stuck his head out the door and growled: "Frater Aelred. Just what in the hell do you think you are doing?"

October 11

If it should happen that a sister is assigned heavy or impossible tasks, let her accept the order of the superior with all gentleness and obedience. But if she thinks that the weight of the task altogether exceeds her strength, she should patiently point out to the superior why she cannot do it. (RB 68.1-2)

This is a surprising little chapter. Of course, it makes perfectly good sense to us to allow a nun to express misgivings about a daunting assignment. But a survey of the previous monastic tradition shows very little background for this idea. True, Basil does allow the monk to question an order, but only grudgingly and as the very last resort (Latin Rule 69 and 82). We should note, however, that Benedict himself seems to assume that the problem is mostly subjective: the nun *thinks* the job is beyond her. The implication is that it is not, but to find that out, she must at least give it a try. There is a good deal of value in this approach because timid personalities tend to see in advance everything that could go wrong. Sometimes they need authority to push them to accomplish scary things.

October 12

The reckoning the abbot must give for others makes him concerned about his own condition. The warnings he gives to others for improvement bring about the correction of his own vices. (RB 2.39-40)

Though it may seem obvious, Benedict does not hesitate to spell out the fact that the abbot's doctrine and directions for the monks are by no means simply meant for others. If his primary task is to guide the community on its journey of spiritual maturation, that process includes himself. In this regard the abbot is not an aloof professional but one of the brothers involved in the same journey. Throughout much of Western monastic history monasteries were saddled with *commendam* abbots: lay people who controlled the abbey revenues but did not live as monks. Often monastic abbots were expected to live at the royal court, so it was natural that they often drifted away from the community. Finally, the Rule itself gives the abbot so much spiritual authority that he may tend to forget that he too needs to live a life of hard striving. When abbots begin to feel that they are exceptional, expect trouble.

October 13

If a brother who has left through his own fault wishes to return to the monastery, he must first promise to thoroughly correct the fault that caused his departure. (RB 29.1)

A departure from the monastery used to be considered to be a fault on the part of the one leaving (see RB 58.28). This was because vows were thought to be unbreakable and/or because society itself allowed no movement from one class or occupation to another. Nowadays the church seems to think that it is better that people not be locked into monastic vows. Moreover, in our society it is very hard for people to risk a final act of commitment, and some of them know they have made a big mistake the minute they make monastic vows. Although we now practice "no fault divorce," before one is allowed back into the community, it is still a good idea to insist on a frank discussion of the issues that precipitated the departure. It could well be that the same dynamics are in place and will simply repeat themselves. Benedict allows up to three returns, but this "in and out" cannot go on forever.

October 14

Because of this love, he can now begin to accomplish effortlessly,
as if spontaneously, everything he previously did out of fear. (RB 7.68)

This statement comes at the end of Benedict's ladder of humility, where he describes the twelve steps as (decreasingly) dependent on fear. His general claim that love is a more powerful motivation than fear is undoubtedly true (see 1 John 4:18). In addition, he brings in the idea of effort and ease. Everyone who has ever learned a skill, or a discipline of any kind, knows that beginnings are always hard. First our synapses and muscles must be trained to new positions and responses, and this can be exceedingly painful and frustrating. But as time goes on, the normal result is increasing ease with the basic technical details. More important, the goal toward which the discipline is aimed, whether it be sport, music or something else, is now attained without much attention to technique. In a sense, true accomplishment begins only at this point. Now one is no longer plodding along, one is flying. Of course, fear and love also involve other dimensions, but they can be compared to discipline and mastery.

October 15

The abbot should knead his orders and teaching into the minds of his
disciples like the leaven of divine justice. (RB 2.5)

The image is of a woman making bread (Matt 13:33): a bit of leaven is worked into the mass of dough so as to permeate it. In this case, "divine justice" could refer to the Bible itself, since it was called the "law of the Lord" in the previous verse. At any rate, it seems reasonable to say that the abbot's *doctrina* should be informed and shaped by serious study of the Bible, to the point that it leavens his own consciousness. Is it taking things too far to claim that the Benedictine abbot's teaching also ought to be relatively brief and unobtrusive like the leaven? Compared to the Rule of the Master, which presents the abbot as a kind of fountain of all wisdom who teaches from morning to night, Benedict's abbot is positively laconic. Still, at least in the United States, communities have more often complained of too little abbatial teaching rather than too much. Exactly how one goes about "kneading it into the minds of the disciples" is another question.

October 16

If we wish to dwell in the tent of his kingdom, we shall not arrive there unless we run by good deeds. (RB Prol. 22)

This verse of the Prologue serves as a transition between the commentary on Psalm 33(34) and Psalm 14(15). Themes from the previous commentary such as "run" and "good deeds" are repeated, but a new element, namely, the "tent," is introduced. The tent was and is a common sight in the Near East, especially among the Bedouin. In Israelite history, the ancestors spent forty years living in tents as desert wanderers. It was a hard time of testing, but it was also a blessed time that was fondly remembered as perhaps their finest hour. Further, this verse speaks of God himself dwelling in a tent. No doubt the reference is to the early moveable covering for the ark of covenant before it found a permanent place in Solomon's Temple in Jerusalem. The constant emphasis of the Prologue on good deeds is balanced off by the idea that the goal of those works is rest in God. Only God can give us access to his dwelling.

October 17

*[Obedient monks] follow the saying of the Lord: "I did not come to do
my own will, but the will of the one who sent me" [John 6:38].*
(RB 5.13)

Some of the biblical texts in chapter 5 compare the abbot to
God or Christ, but John 6:38 compares the *monk* to Christ:
although he was the Savior of the World, he was first all the
obedient Son of the Father. In other words, along with being
obedient *to* Christ, the monk ought to be obedient *together with*
Christ. Someone might object that it is all well and good to
urge us to be obedient like Christ. But if he really was one with
the Father, as he claims throughout the Gospel of John, then he
knew God's will perfectly and experienced no sinful tendencies to go against it. (The temptations of Christ suggest that his
obedience was not a cut and dried matter.) The same cannot be
said for us! In this sense, our road of obedience might be said
to be rockier than Christ's—except that it does not usually lead
to crucifixion. We ought to pray for the obedient Christ to accompany us on our sometimes tortuous way of obedience.

October 18

*He will do this no longer out of fear of hell, but out of love for Christ,
good habit and delight in virtue.* (RB 7.69)

At the end of the ladder of humility, Benedict enunciates what
appears to be a perfectly straightforward idea. Yet a study of
his sources reveals a considerable amount of development. The
original formulation of John Cassian speaks only of "love for

the good in itself" (*Inst.* 4.39). While it is true that he also yokes this with "love for Christ," he does not say so here. The Master expands this by adding "good habit and delight in virtue" (RM 10.90). Although this says a lot, it still does not say enough, so Benedict adds the name of Christ, thus providing a Christian seal to the whole chapter on humility. As a matter of fact, this chapter rarely speaks of Christ, no doubt assuming his presence in the whole ascetic process as do all the church fathers. But Benedict is not satisfied with that. And we can say there is always danger of the monastic "ideology" drifting away from the basic message of Jesus' teaching and life. We are Christians before we are monks.

October 19

Let the greatest care be taken when receiving the poor and pilgrims, for in them is Christ especially received. For the very fear of the rich guarantees them respect. (RB 53.15)

As obvious as this seems to us today, it has not been easy to observe throughout monastic history. For example, we have the floor plan of an elaborate guesthouse in the early Middle Ages (Plan of St. Gall) indicating that the rich and the poor guests had completely separate quarters. No doubt they were treated very differently. Perhaps that was unavoidable, given the nature of the feudal system. It is not so today. Monasteries have to remain sensitive to the faith dimension of their relation to the outside world. If we really believe that Christ is especially received in the poor and pilgrims, we will be very hesitant to treat them carelessly. They are used to it; that is the way the world treats them. But when they come to the monastery, usually in some kind of need, they deserve better from us. Not because they are attractive; often they are anything but! Yet Benedict insists that Christ loves them most of all.

October 20

Sisters who are working very far from the oratory, and cannot arrive there on time, should pray the Office where they are at work. When they are sent on a journey, they should not omit praying at the appropriate times. (RB 50 1, 3-4)

In this little chapter, Benedict enunciates a fairly important principle: prayer is not tied to place or circumstance. Just because the sister finds herself outside of the usual parameters of her life, this does not excuse her from prayer. What is more, she is not simply free to make her *own* form of prayer. Later in the chapter Benedict speaks of their "debt of service" *(pensum servitutis)*, which seems to imply an objective obligation to official prayer. Yet changed circumstances obviously will usually suggest modifications in the prayer practices. Thus the sisters are told to kneel at prayer out in the fields, but that is probably not appropriate on public conveyances. Still, the spectacle of a Muslim unfurling his prayer rug in the aisle of a 747 jet can make others think. The religious who declines to wear the habit on a plane may avoid some uncomfortable questions, but she also loses a chance to witness to her vocation.

October 21

They should love their prioress with sincere and humble charity.
(RB 72.10)

Like 1 Corinthians 13, chapter 72 rings the changes of love. Finally we come to the question: how should we love the superior? Some sisters might be surprised by the very idea.

Aren't we suppose to obey her? Who can ask more? Well, in fact Benedict does. Or at least he tells the prioress to "seek to be loved rather than feared" (RB 64.15). Now that can go too far. It was said that Bill Clinton's besetting fault was that he wanted everyone to love him; it caused him to do some very unwise things. But if we demand that sisters should love their prioress, we should be aware that such love is always vulnerable to corruption by power. By that I mean that the sisters are still dependent and therefore could be tempted to feign affection. That's why Benedict makes sure to specify that this particular love should be sincere. There is no place here for sycophancy. For that, see the Rule of the Master, chapter 91. Finally, Benedict certainly does not ask the sisters to love the prioress as their mother. They are not little girls; they are grownup daughters.

October 22

When we wish to propose something to powerful people, we do not presume to do so without humility and reverence. (RB 20.1)

It wasn't right. The prefects in the school were loaded down with work, and yet the prior had the nerve to appoint Father Gervase to be master of ceremonies at the Pontifical High Mass on December 8th (the solemnity of the Immaculate Conception of Mary). Gervase hated these Pontificals. They were full of bowing and curtsying, and there was always tension when people made their inevitable mistakes. Besides, the master of ceremonies was in charge of the whole shebang, but Gervase had no time at all to review the ceremonies. In fact, he came running in just before the Mass, to the great annoyance of Abbot Stephen. The first thing that Gervase had to do was to vest the abbot in front of the high altar—as if a grown man couldn't dress himself! But Gervase was no valet, and he managed to mess up the abbot's long, blond hair by forgetting to unsnap the chasuble at the top. "Have you got a comb? You should practice this stuff!" said the abbot under his breath. After Mass, Gervase showed up at the abbot's door with a chasuble for practice. "Get out of my sight!" roared the abbot.

October 23

If a sister thinks the weight of the task altogether exceeds her strength, she should patiently point out to the superior why she cannot do it. She should do so at an appropriate time, without pride, resistance or refusal. (RB 68.2-3)

Of course, one would approach such a discussion in a patient, humble manner—wouldn't one? Not necessarily. Some people are not good at all in these kinds of transactions. They tend to oscillate between aggression and obsequiousness. Perhaps they have not learned to negotiate hard matters with their parents. Now they repeat this behavior with the prioress. One gets the impression that Benedict is just as interested in the process here as he is in the substance. For if there to be a healthy tone to monastic obedience, it must be characterized by calmness, frankness, gentleness—just the opposite from the wonderful Latin trio of *non superbiendo aut resistendo vel contradicendo* (pride, resistance or refusal). And even if one finds oneself in the extreme situation of having to resist an order, one should learn to do it nonviolently.

October 24

Let there be profound silence in the refectory, so that the only voice heard there is that of the reader and not of anyone else whispering or talking. (RB 38.5)

Since Benedict requires that there be table reading at most meals, he also wishes to create a proper ambience for such reading. Obviously, that suggests silence, and not just any silence but the "most profound" kind. In a sense, that is impossible since a group of people cannot eat without making some noise. But what Benedict really does not want is commentary on the reading, even in a low voice. It is easier to understand his point if we take into account chapter 24 of the Rule of the Master. There we find something very different: a veritable ongoing seminar with the monks asking questions about the reading and the abbot discoursing freely on the same. That is not unusual in the Rule of the Master, which seems to see the abbot as a kind of guru who teaches all day long. As verses 8–9 make clear, Benedict does not want that. It is enough simply to eat in silence and listen to the word of God read aloud.

October 25

Therefore, regarding children or youths or those who do not understand the seriousness of excommunication, when these people misbehave, they should be deprived of food or beaten with sharp blows to correct them. (RB 30.2)

We are puzzled by the very presence of children in Benedict's monastery, but we should note that the Latin terms employed *(pueri, adulescentes)* can vary a lot in their parameters. Another barrier to insight here could lie in our repugnance to corporal punishment, and especially in a religious setting. Yet most traditional societies thought there are times when children need to be paddled. A third problem seems to lie in a confusion about child psychology. Who says that children do not suffer from ostracization? Some societies (for example, North American Plains Indians) regularly discipline their youth in this fashion. But after clearing aside these anomalies, we are left here with a perfectly valid idea: You cannot punish people by depriving them of that which they do not value! Consequently, in our individualistic Western culture excommunication seems to lose much of its force. To remain healthy, the monastic community in every age must develop its own body of sanctions that will protect it from destructive behavior.

October 26

The abbot should know that the shepherd will bear the blame if the owner of the sheep finds them less than healthy. (RB 2.7)

In this scenario, the abbot is the shepherd and God is the owner of the sheep, that is, the monastic community. This arrangement is very familiar to the New Testament and even in our own day in the American West. Applied to the monastic life, it is a rather hard teaching that denies the abbot "ownership" of the community, yet places a very heavy responsibility upon him. In fact, this theme—the abbot's heavy responsibility—is repeated over and over in this chapter, so much so that it is a wonder that anyone would dare to undertake the office. It seems clear from this verse that the abbot has obligations both to the community and to God. His position midway between these two poles can seem crushing at times, but he should remember that his concern is also very simple: the health of the sheep. If he can keep that in mind, he will be less liable to get sidetracked with "minor" issues such as how to pay the bills.

October 27

"The person who walks without blame and acts justly; who candidly speaks the truth and has not used his tongue to deceive; who does no evil to his neighbor" [Ps 14(15):2-3]. (RB Prol. 25-27)

These verses of the Prologue are in answer to the question: "Lord, who will live in your tent, or who will rest on your holy mountain?" from Psalm 14(15). It is clear that the answer is totally practical: dwelling with God is only open to one who lives a life of practical virtue. This is completely characteristic of the Hebrew Bible, which is eminently down to earth in its spirituality: all that really counts is to obey the commandments of the Lord, which demand justice towards the other members of the community. It is interesting, but perhaps coincidental, that sins of the tongue are condemned both here and in Psalm 33(34):14. Still, it can be said that in a small, isolated community such as an Israelite village or a Benedictine monastery, it is especially important that persons refrain from wounding one another with sharp remarks. Yet this does not rule out the need for candor in speech, which tries to tell the truth—but not brutally.

October 28

Obedience will only be acceptable to God . . . if it be given gladly by disciples. For "God loves a cheerful giver" [2 Cor 9:7]. (RB 5.14, 16)

This chapter on obedience is not "politically correct." It flies in the face of the modern sensibility by demanding uncompromising, instantaneous obedience to the abbot. Part of the toughness here comes from compressing a much longer chapter in the Rule of the Master in such a way that only the harsh essentials remain. But it is still not correct to dismiss monastic obedience as something better suited to the army than the church. Most people don't join the army voluntarily, they are conscripted. Therefore, who can blame them if their obedience is grudging and sometimes even subversive? Indeed, outside of battle, common soldiers pride themselves on "foot dragging." In the kingdom of God, however, things are quite different. No one is here against his will, and no one can coerce him to do anything. Therefore, anything but spontaneous, joyous obedience is not only illogical but spiritually counterproductive. Indeed, Benedict is not afraid to declare that mere material obedience (simply going through the motions) is worthless.

October 29

So the Lord says in the Gospel: "Whoever hears these words of mine and puts them into practice, I would compare to a wise person who built his house on rock. The rains came, the wind howled and battered his house, but it did not collapse because it was built on rock" [Matt 7:24-25].
(RB Prol. 33-34)

Although it is not an obvious choice, this text is used by Benedict to comment on Psalm 14(15):1-4. The Psalmist and the Master, but not Benedict, admonish the hearer to avoid oaths, usury and bribes. But Benedict joins them in concluding: "Whoever does these things shall never be moved." This then calls to his mind the passage in Matthew where the prudent person builds her house on an immovable rock. Since Christ the Rock was mentioned a few verses previously, it is not unreasonable to import the same image into this verse. Sometimes in very poor countries, a heavy rain causes the jerry-built shacks to collapse in the mudslides. Likewise, Matthew warns that anyone who hears the Lord's words but does not put them into practice risks precisely this kind of catastrophe. Christ is only a rock of stability for those who obey his words.

October 30

A sister who is sent on some errand, and is expected to return to the monastery on the same day, should not presume to eat outside. This is so even if she is begged to do so by someone, unless that someone is the prioress. (RB 51.1-2)

Why is it so bad for a religious to eat outside the monastery? To get some insight into the thinking on display here, we have to remember that in ancient times meals were much more symbolically charged than they are for us. Everything hinged on who you ate with, and when. Consequently, there really were no casual meals. Secondly, it is likely that the "someone" who is begging the sister to eat on the road is in fact her family. Now, one of the most difficult things for them was to cut their ties to their families and join a new family, the family of Benedict, the family of Christ. One did not do this by dining at home. No doubt our own relation to the outside world is different, but it is still not casual.

October 31

They should fear God out of love. (RB 72.9)

This is the shortest verse in the Rule—three Latin words *(amore deum timeant)*. But it used to have only two words *(Deum timeant)* before scholars demonstrated that *amore* belongs to this, not the previous sentence. Why had the scribes separated them? Probably because the very idea of fearing God out of love made little sense to them. We probably also have trouble with it, for love seems to be the antithesis of fear. Yet in the Bible it is not. In fact, when the Jewish Bible wants to describe a perfectly pious Jew, it says that she is full of "fear of the Lord" (see Deut 10:12). Some people object that for them fear means something like reverential awe. Very well, but the two ideas are also close in the English language. Since chapter 72 is all about love, this verse simply describes another form of love, perhaps the highest kind of all. As Christians, we know that God first loves and we are to respond with love for God. But since God is God, we also know that this loving relation must never become a familiarity that breeds contempt.

November 1

One who arrives at the monastery at the second hour should realize that he is junior to one who arrived at the first hour, no matter what his age or status. (RB 63.8)

At St. Joseph Abbey, they had big novitiates. In addition to their own crowd of novices, they usually had novices from other abbeys. And so the novitiate was like a small community unto itself. Like the rest of the abbey, the novices had a "pecking order" that was established by time of entry. Of course, most of them showed up for school on the same day, so there wasn't much to choose, but the novice master, Father Athanasius, did his best to determine the right order. Still, he was wise enough to see that this system could cause problems in such a closed environment so it needed some adjustments. One year Frater Roger was the senior novice and he was a problem. From the beginning, he lorded it over the others, claiming for himself prerogatives guaranteed to irritate everybody. At the end of his first week, Father Athanasius announced to the group: "One thing I forgot to mention. This is a rotation system: at the end of each week, the senior novice goes to end of the line."

November 2

If the superior does not change her mind or her order, even after her suggestion, the junior should realize that it is best for her. Then, trusting in the help of God, she should obey out of love. (RB 68.4-5)

This is the ending of the little chapter on questioning hard obedience, and it may be a disappointment for us. We may suspect that it is just another example of the way monastic authority always seems to win its battles. That would be a false impression; Benedict surely does not see it as a power struggle. He sees it as an opportunity for growth for the individual. Except where one cannot obey for reasons of conscience—a case that few monastics ever have to experience—one never goes wrong by obeying. It may cost a great deal, but it helps a lot to know that I am not alone. God is my helper in all this. Notice especially the last word of the quote: *love.* Because God so loved us (even to the death of the cross), we can now do "impossible" things for the community. And sometimes superiors change their minds.

November 3

On all Sundays outside of Lent, the canticles, Matins, Prime, Terce, Sext and None are said with Alleluia. (RB 15.3)

We may be tempted to overlook a liturgical detail such as this one. In itself it is quite unremarkable, but in comparison with the greater church it is not, for the rest of the church (outside of the Roman West) did not use Alleluia in this manner outside of the Easter season. So the monks used Alleluia more than anyone else (except the Greek church, which uses it even during Lent!). Isn't that a bit odd, since Benedict says our whole existence should have a Lenten quality (RB 49.1)? Perhaps not. The ancient monks felt they were already living the *angelikos bios*, the heavenly life. Granted, monastic life seems anything but "heavenly" on most Monday mornings, but we are a little like the angels who "do not marry or give in marriage" (see Mark 12:25). And we have a special obligation to live as "Easter people."

November 4

If some of the craftwork is to be marketed, those who carry out the transaction should not dare to engage in any deception . . . The scourge of avarice ought not to creep into these prices . . . They should charge a little less than seculars can "so that God may be glorified in all things" [1 Pet 4:11]. (RB 57.4, 7-8)

Sad to say, "the scourge of avarice" has often driven monastic economic policies, and that was even the case in the so-called golden age. One is appalled by the hard-nosed economic methods employed by the medieval monks. Whole villages were dispersed so the monks could run sheep there. Abbots spent much of their time in court battling for the economic advantage of the monastery. And yet economics is a complex and subtle subject, and sometimes simple principles are not enough either. Take the matter of slightly underselling seculars. Benedict suggests this for spiritual purposes, but it might look a bit different to our secular competitors! It will not do to woodenly apply ancient ideals to the concrete circumstances of modern life. Avarice may just be masquerading as virtue.

November 5

[The monastic cellarer] should be a wise person, mature in character and well disciplined. He should not be gluttonous, arrogant, violent, hurtful, stingy or wasteful. (RB 31.1)

St. Benedict's cellarer (business manager) is one of the most important officials in the monastery. Indeed, some scholars believe that at an early stage of Benedict's monastery, the cellarer may have been the *only* official after the abbot. Unlike his counterpart in the Rule of the Master (RM 16), this cellarer is not a mere functionary but a highly responsible collaborator with the abbot. This point is made in many ways, but in this verse it is done by a series of adjectives that resemble those applied to the abbot himself in chapter 64 (vv. 16-18). Obviously, one who is wise, mature and well disciplined is fit for general leadership, including spiritual guidance. The Master emphasizes the need for the cellarer to avoid self-indulgence, and that is also true of Benedict. But the latter also extends the discussion to issues such as violence *(turbulentus)*, which have more to do with the proper treatment of persons. Clearly, this job is not simply about balancing budgets. Only grown-ups need apply.

November 6

When his worker has been cleansed of vices and sins, then the Lord will graciously make all this shine forth in him through the Holy Spirit. (RB 7.70)

This is one of the few times that Benedict mentions the Holy Spirit. But what role does he give to the third person of the Trinity? To tell the truth, it is not so crystal clear. For the Latin grammar could be construed to make the Holy Spirit the one who "cleanses the worker of vices and sins" or the one who makes love shine forth in the monk, as we have translated it here. This is no place to discuss the grammatical reasons for choosing one or the other interpretation, but we can give the theological reasoning. To limit the Holy Spirit to the ascetic purification of the monk in humility seems an unbiblical reduction of her role in the Christian life. It is also not helpful to suggest that the Holy Spirit only enters the picture once we have been purified of sin. Our entire sanctification is wrought by the Holy Spirit received by us in baptism and active in our hearts throughout the Christian life.

November 7

If the shepherd has devoted all his concern to a restless and disobedient flock . . . the sheep will receive punishment for rejecting his care: death will overtake them. (RB 2.8, 10)

Chapter 2 loads a lot of responsibility on the abbot, perhaps more than most people are willing to bear. But it does not absolve the monks of their share of the load. In the direst possible language Benedict warns them that cenobitic life is no sinecure: unless they obey the abbot, they are risking damnation. When a group of monks comes to one of its periodical abbatial elections, it should ask itself: Do we actually *want* an abbot? Are we ready and willing to follow where he leads us? Are we prone to withdraw allegiance from him the first time he asks us for hard things? Yet it must also be remembered that mere passive acquiescence is not enough. A community may abdicate its responsibility just as culpably by refusing to share in decision making and in serious discernment. Taken to its logical conclusion, this leaves the abbot the only full moral agent in the community, a situation not acceptable to Benedict.

November 8

When the wicked one, the devil, suggests something to him, he pushes him and his advice out of the sight of his heart. (RB Prol. 28)

This is the first mention of the devil in the Rule, and in fact one of the few times Benedict speaks of the wicked one at all. This may not seem particularly significant to a modern reader who rarely even thinks of Satan, but it is worth noticing. A comparison with the Rule of the Master, which is Benedict's prototype, shows that for the Master, the devil is of extreme importance. Indeed, the Master concedes rulership of the world to the devil; for the Master, one comes to the monastery primarily to flee the wicked one. Benedict is hardly that pessimistic about the power of Satan. He takes it seriously, as in this verse, but does not exaggerate it. Note that the wicked one is actively seeking to bring the monk down, but he can be pushed aside by a person who is ready and willing to do so. Cassiodorus makes a helpful connection when he invokes Mark 8:33: "Christ reduces him to nothing in his sight when he says: 'Get behind me, Satan; you shall not tempt the Lord your God.'"

November 9

"I will guard my ways that I sin not with my tongue. I placed a barrier at my mouth. I was speechless and humbled, refraining even from good speech." [Ps 38(39):2-3]. (RB 6.1)

St. Benedict, following the Master, uses these psalm verses as the biblical warrant for his teaching on silence: if the psalmist refrained even from good words, how much more ought we refrain from evil ones! It is a perfectly reasonable piece of moralism, but it finds little basis in the psalm itself. The Bible never teaches that total abstinence from speech is a virtuous thing. That is a monastic point of view with later roots, perhaps in Greek philosophy. The fact that the old monks felt free to bend the psalm text slightly to make their point should not surprise us. For one thing, these people spent so much time with the biblical text that they apparently felt a deep sense of freedom with it. What is more, they assumed that their own ascetical philosophy was totally consonant with the Bible. Be that as it may, we must remember that Christian monasticism must be based on what the Bible actually says, not what we wish it said.

November 10

Reading should not be lacking at the meals of the brothers, nor should it be done by just anyone who happens to pick up the book. (RB 38.1)

In his typical fashion, Benedict begins chapter 38 with a statement of principle, actually a double principle: In the monastery, there must be reading at table and it should be well done. Good table reading demands a competent performance by the reader. Anything else can be a cause of indigestion. Because ancient manuscripts were so poorly punctuated, it was particularly necessary for the reader to prepare for public performance. Done properly, table reading is a valuable piece of monastic culture. Table reading has been used in monasteries for so many centuries, it is not often remembered that this is a rather unusual practice. After all, what is more humane than good talk at table? To abolish such a universally beloved practice would seem to demand a truly weighty reason. Probably the ancient monks felt that the Bible outweighed just about anything, so no reasons needed to be given.

November 11

Let the oratory be in fact what it is called, and let nothing else be done or stored there . . . Whoever is not busy with this kind of work (private prayer) after the Work of God, is not permitted to remain in the oratory, as the place is called. (RB 52.1, 5)

These verses, the first and last of chapter 52, make the same point: the oratory is a place for prayer and nothing else. That may seem like a truism to us, but this was not always so. In the monastic tradition before Benedict, and especially with Pachomius, it was customary to bring weaving to the Divine Office. Sisters mainly listened to psalms and reading, while keeping busy with their hands. There is a certain psychological realism in that practice. At least it beats dozing! But for Benedict it still was not a good idea. No, he wants the oratory to be strictly what it is called, a place for prayer *(orare)*. This type of argument, that things should actually *be* what they are *called*, is very typical of Benedict. It marks him as a person who is quite sensitive to jargon that says anything but what it actually means.

November 12

They should offer selfless love to the sisters. (RB 72.8)

Benedict commands the sisters to love each other *caste,* which used to be translated "chastely." It goes without saying that religious with promises of perpetual chastity should live thus. Yet, *caste* has little to do with erotic relations; instead it refers to pure motives. That means that the love between sisters is to be selfless, not possessive. In former times the sisters were warned about "particular friendships," which mostly meant pairing up. In recent times it has been pointed out that *all* friendships are particular. Nevertheless, this admonition had some value, and it still has some value. If we take it to be warning against exploitative relationships, it is well worth heeding. Of course, some people find this more difficult than others. Such persons are "users" of others, perhaps by temperament. For them this verse is particularly salutary, but it also has general value. A community bound together by selfless love is the strongest kind of community imaginable.

November 13

When they address one another, no one is permitted to call another by his simple name. (RB 63.11)

The interview was not going well. The abbot always found it hard to talk to Brother James, who seemed to have an authority problem. Even though he was a senior monk, he never learned to open himself up to the abbot, no matter who the abbot happened to be. On this particular day, for example, he actually came into the office armed with a fly swatter and proceeded to flail away while the abbot was trying to make a few points. "Do you understand what I am trying to say, Jim?" said the abbot. "No, I don't. You always use big words that I can't understand. And I don't want you calling me Jim. Benedict says that's not right." Later in the day, Brother James had to go into town shopping and that brought him to Johnson's Hardware Store. He liked Tom Johnson, who was always cheerful and accepting of him. "Hi, Jim!" he shouted from the back of the store. Jim beamed.

November 14

It is especially to be avoided that anyone in the monastery defend another or take her under her wing on any occasion. This applies even if they are members of the same family. (RB 69.1-2)

This tiny chapter is not one of Benedict's better-known creations. Nevertheless, anyone who has ever lived in a close-knit human community knows that it is very relevant. The problem usually does not come from blood relationships. In the "good old days" there were plenty of these family ties in our American monasteries, but people knew well enough that the Rule does not permit nepotism. A larger problem, and one that will persist as long as original sin, is the need some people have to control other people. Of course, Benedict is talking here about tutelage in which a powerful person seems to protect a weaker one. This protection is almost always just a pretense for control. To be the object of such protection is far worse than being without it. Wherever monastic authority comes upon these cases, they must be dealt with summarily. Those who have a need to control the lives of others should be offered help, but they may have to be disciplined.

November 15

Taking into account the weaknesses of various persons, we believe that two cooked dishes are enough for the daily meal at all times of the year, whether at the sixth or ninth hour. For someone who cannot eat one dish may be able to eat the other. (RB 39.1-2)

Benedict is not a totalitarian thinker but a nuanced one. Once upon a time a would-be monastic founder reasoned that it would be best to find an ideal food and then serve only that to his monks. So he hired a dietitian who concocted "brownies" containing seaweed, vitamins and so on, and that is all they ate. After some time, all the monks left. Benedict knows this cannot work. Even if one imposes a rigid and narrow cuisine, people will multiply "exceptions." It is best to offer enough variety to accommodate a spectrum of persons. This principle has considerable validity throughout the entire gamut of community life: there must be some "wiggle room." Although Benedict seems to call human variety a "weakness" in this chapter, that is not the only possible translation.

November 16

If there are skilled workers in the monastery, let them practice their craft with all humility and with the prioress' permission. But if anyone of these workers is so proud of her expertise that she thinks she is a great gift to the monastery, she should be removed from her job. (RB 57.1-3)

The situation in these verses is no mystery. Monasteries are typically full of skilled people, and skilled people are normally proud of their skills. That is a psychological fact of life, and not a mere shame. But Benedict wants his craftsmen to be characterized by humility. In this case, are pride and humility mutually exclusive? I don't think so. Note that Benedict does not advocate the *humiliation* of the craftsmen. That is what we do to them if we deny them proper tools, proper materials, proper support. What we must never do is to force them into shoddy work. For a true craftsman, that is the ultimate humiliation. Yet it must be admitted that artists and high-level craftsmen sometimes have a hard time in the monastery. They are often so sensitive that they find the common life very burdensome. And most burdensome of all is to have one's art misunderstood.

November 17

[The cellarer] should be a person who fears God and is like the father [abbot] to the whole community. (RB 31.2)

It is no accident that Benedict requires that the cellarer be "God-fearing" *(timens Deum)*. This is a quality that he wants in all monastic officials (see RB 36.7; 53.21), but especially those who deal with powerless persons. How is this so in the case of the cellarer? Every cenobite has taken a vow of poverty in which he or she forswears personal property. Therefore, every cenobite is radically dependent on the community for the means of physical life: food, shelter, clothing and so on. Now the cellarer is the official whose task it is to care for these needs and Benedict wants this work done in the "fear of God," although man does not live by theology alone. The abbot must also operate in this manner and the cellarer must stand in for him in many practical transactions. This does not mean that there is a clear division of labor in a Benedictine monastery, with the abbot handling the spiritual and the cellarer, the material. The bottom line here is *not* hard-fisted economics.

November 18

The time that remains after Vigils should be used for the learning of psalms and lessons by those brothers who are lacking in this matter. (RB 8.3)

During the winter, the ancient monastic schedule left a certain amount of time between the Matins and Lauds, and Benedict says that this time is be spent in "learning" psalms and lessons. That could refer to study, but most likely it refers to memorizing these materials. They were memorized specifically for use in the Divine Office, which was done largely by heart in those days. An important by-product of this process was to stock the memory of the monk with holy texts, which could then be called forth at will for personal meditation ("rumination"). The memories of persons in the days before printing were much more extensive than our own. Pachomius thinks nothing of requiring that the postulant memorize the entire psalter before entry into the monastic choir. Pachomian brothers were expected to murmur and meditate the verses of the Bible as they worked or moved from place to place (Rule of Pachomius, 59–60).

November 19

The abbot can teach gifted disciples the Lord's commands by his words, but he will have to model personally the divine precepts to the stubborn or the simple. (RB 2.12)

Apparently Benedict took for granted that there would usually be both clever and dull people among his monks. However in the verses that follow, it becomes clear that he actually believes that *all* persons respond best to lived example. Of course, the clever can more easily distinguish between the person and the message of the teacher, but deep down, we all want to see authenticity in our teachers. And especially in a "wisdom teacher" such as an abbot, whose only real expertise lies in the area of holy living. Still, as long as it is true that all of us are sinners and that someone must teach (lead), we have to be ready to forgive the superior his sins. Unless he is a complete hypocrite, every religious teacher knows he is preaching to himself first of all. Once, when Louis XV upbraided his prime minister for immoral conduct, the latter said: "What about yourself?" "I, of course, am a special case" said Louis.

November 20

He annihilates these thoughts, taking them and smashing them against Christ while they are still little [Ps 136(137):9]. (RB Prol. 28)

When discussing resistance to temptation, Benedict invokes Psalm 136(137). In doing so, he was following many of the church fathers, but that does not make the reference any less shocking. For Psalm 136(137) speaks of the barbaric military custom of massacring infants. Still, if we can overcome our initial revulsion, this can prove to be a fruitful image when applied to "thoughts." In this context, "thoughts" means harmful thoughts, what the Greeks called *logismoi.* Much spiritual direction in the monastic deserts of the East involved revealing such "thoughts" to the director for inspection. The great benefit of such candor lies in exposing them to the scrutiny of an objective judge who can help us root them out before they fester and grow into obsessions (see RB 4.50). But the imagery employed here is even more powerful, since we are urged to smash them "against Christ." Surely this is one of the least lovely references to Christ in all of patristic literature, but it is highly effective. Perhaps the allusion is to Christ the Rock (1 Cor 10:4).

November 21

Due to the intrinsic value of silence itself, perfect disciples should rarely be granted permission to speak, even good, holy and edifying words. (RB 6.2-3)

These are very difficult verses to translate. To make them work, one must find "surplus meaning" in *taciturnitas,* which we here render "intrinsic value of silence." This seems to imply that there are different kinds of silence, some of it merely material, some moral and some almost mystical. Apparently, the reference here is to the highest form of silence. This still does not adequately explain the puzzling remark that "perfect" disciples should allowed even less speech than other monks, which seems to invert the biblical idea of freedom of speech for the children of God. The very term "perfect" disciple is a remnant from the Rule of the Master that Benedict has retained, even though he abandons the rest of an elaborate schema in which the more perfect have the least freedom (RM 8–9). In fact, casual remarks throughout Benedict's Rule (see chapters 42 and 49) indicate that Benedict allowed ordinary speech in his monastery. The suppression of *all* speech only appears in the Trappist reform of Abbot de Rancé in the seventeenth century.

November 22

The books read at Vigils should be of divine authority, whether of the Old or New Testament. The biblical commentaries of well-known and trustworthy Catholic fathers may also be used. (RB 9.8)

Apparently Benedict is quite concerned about what is read to his monks at the Divine Office. He says it should be of "divine authority," which refers to the books of the Bible. Some monasteries today read only Scripture at the Office, but others take a broader approach to the subject. In doing this, they are also following the Holy Rule, which allows that reliable biblical commentaries might be used in addition to the Bible itself. In attempting to define what makes a commentary trustworthy, Benedict says it is written by "well-known and trustworthy Catholic fathers." But how does a commentary become well known if it is not read for the first time? And what is a Catholic father for our day and age? One of the most notable characteristics of current Catholic biblical scholarship is its inclusivity. For the first time female scholars, scholars from the southern hemisphere and other minorities are being heard. Would this please Benedict? It would if those new commentators aid us in penetrating Scripture in new ways. And they do.

November 23

He should consider the utensils and goods of the monastery as if they were the consecrated vessels of the altar. He should treat nothing as negligible. (RB 31.10)

One almost hesitates to add any more commentary to one of the most heavily commented verses in the entire Rule of Benedict. Still, in our throwaway culture, the verse sticks out like a counter-cultural sore thumb. Of course, it applies to everyone, not just the cellarer. But if he does not set a good example in this matter, then he will have neglected an important part of his job. In a world where everything is treated as a commodity to be exploited, it is a constant battle to promote reverence for material creation. Some people may come into the monastery deeply imbued with the "new ethic." In direct contradistinction to their frugal elders (formed in the days of the Depression and the Dust Bowl), they seem to deliberately waste resources. How to transmit the value of monastic frugality? But there is reason for hope since more and more young people are becoming convinced that the future of the planet depends on reverence.

November 24

If someone wishes to pray privately at some other time, she should simply go in and pray. Let her do so, not in a loud voice, but with tears and full attention of heart. (RB 52.4)

In the verse preceding this, Benedict warns those exiting the Divine Office to do so quietly so as not to disturb those who remain to pray in private. Here he asks the one praying to do so in a quiet manner and not in a "loud voice." It is hard for us to imagine private prayer "in a loud voice," but that is because we have not spent time in the temples of Africa and Asia. There, people are much less inhibited in these matters, and they also seem better able to tolerate more noise and clatter than we are. In that sense, Benedict is more like we are than he is like they are. He wants to create a very quiet atmosphere for prayer in the oratory. He thinks that full concentration needs and deserves that kind of context. He also thinks it will be conducive to tears, which are for him a sign of genuine prayer. By and large, Catholic churches the world over remain places where one can do just this.

November 25

No one should pursue what she judges helpful to herself, but rather what is useful to others. (RB 72.7)

If this sounds too good to be true, if it sounds otherworldly —well, it is straight out of the New Testament. In Philippians 2:4, just before the magnificent christological hymn, we find the same injunction. To give it a high-fallutin' title, it is "radical altruism." It is the polar opposite of typical capitalist thinking, which claims that the best way to help others is to help yourself. It is also the contradiction of original sin wherein we live for others rather than for ourselves. It might be noted that many serious thinkers believe that the only way to true self-realization is to live for others. In other words, there is no direct way to become one's truest self except by putting aside that same self on behalf of others. Surely this is the deep significance of Jesus' assurance that "She who wishes to save her life will lose it. But whoever loses her life for my sake and that of the Gospel, will save it" (see Mark 8.35). Even the final word, "useful," is laden with meaning, for it means that we are concerned first of all for the common good.

November 26

*We read that wine is absolutely not for monks. But since monks in
our day cannot be convinced of this, let us at least agree not to drink
to excess, but sparingly. For "wine makes even the wise go astray."*
(RB 40.6-7)

Unloading the wine truck was a big job. The cases weighed
about 40 pounds and there were at least a thousand of them.
Fortunately, though, "many hands make light work," and there
were many hands in St. Charles Abbey. Furthermore, there was
something inspiring about the sight of a long line of brothers
each carrying cases to the wine cellar. Afterward, the wine
master would reward the group with a bottle of good table
wine for their trouble. As the job came to an end one afternoon,
Brother Julius noticed Father Mark carrying a case of wine like
the rest. That was odd, since he was usually nowhere to be seen.
In fact, he was a closet alcoholic, and Julius knew it. To his
amusement, the gift bottle for the group ended up in Mark's
hands. "Don't try to drink this stuff straight, fellas," said Mark,
"it could harm your liver."

November 27

*Every occasion for arbitrary behavior must be blocked in the monastery.
Therefore, we decree that no one is permitted to excommunicate one of
her sisters or strike her unless the prioress has given her that power.*
(RB 70.1-2)

We do not ordinarily condone physical punishment of
others, even of children. There seems to be no question that

Benedict lived in a more physical age, and that the emotions of medieval people were nearer the surface than ours. Perhaps he had some fairly "primitive" Goths in his community. At least he feels it is necessary to deal firmly with the possibility of unauthorized physical punishment. But does this still speak to us? It is quite important to recognize that our violence may lie buried deeper, but it is still there. The main issue here is not the physical, but the arbitrary. Benedict is a person of order; there is nothing that offends him more than hijacked or wildcat authority. For someone to punish on her own authority, probably assuming she is God's instrument of choice, is to undermine the very foundations of order in the community. Such a person must be firmly put back in place.

November 28

Let two dishes suffice for all the brothers, but a third may be added if fruit or fresh vegetables are in season. A generous pound weight of bread should be enough for the day . . . If the workload becomes heavy, the abbot may decide that more food should be added. (RB 39.3)

It may strike the modern reader that Benedict is not particularly rigorous about fasting. Certainly, two or three cooked dishes plus a pound of bread was by no means a starvation diet. When Benedict wants to impose discipline at table, he simply has them eat later in the day. In the lives of many of the saints, we read that they practiced remarkable degrees of fasting. We also read that many of them ruined their health in the process. Benedict seems to prefer that his people maintain their health in a moderate fashion, so they can serve one another and also succor the poor. John Cassian agrees, noting that there is absolutely no spiritual profit to be found in fasting to the point that one is then driven to overindulgence—much better to maintain a reasonable, sustainable level of nutrition for the long haul (*Conf.* 2.18-24).

November 29

The prioress should always ponder the Acts of the Apostles: "Each person used to receive what was needed" [Acts 4.35]. Therefore, the prioress should pay attention to the needs of the weak ones, not the bad will of the envious ones. (RB 55.20-21)

These verses close the chapter on "The Clothing and Footwear of the Sisters." One of Benedict's main points in that chapter is that the members of the monastic community not help themselves to goods, and also that they not hoard what they have received. Benedict teaches a rather severe form of dispossession. But the other side of that coin is this: Monastic authority must take care of people. It must provide them with what they need—which is not always what they want. For if the nuns do not receive what they need, they will be tempted to *take care of themselves.* Now this is the American ideal, to take care of yourself. But it is a monastic bane. When we come upon a situation where nuns are mishandling possessions, we ought to ask ourselves whether this is a result of the prevalent vice of avarice, or is it because the authority has not taken proper care of them?

November 30

[The cellarer] should not aggravate the brothers. If someone should demand something in a rough way, he should not crush him with a rebuke, but deny the tactless request in a calm and gentle way.
(RB 31.6-7)

Someone might be scandalized that monks get into conflicts, but it is well to remember they are still sinners. Furthermore, not all of them even know how to express themselves in a gentle way. That has to be taken into account when dealing with them, but one should also understand that some people find it quite hard to ask for what they need.

When Father Christopher was resisting reassignment from a parish to the monastery, he put it this way: "I don't want to have to ask the abbot for a nickel for a popsicle!" It would be easy enough to say that such monks just "don't get it," but that's too simple. Benedict knows this life is not easy and he does not want to see any more "sadness" *(tristitia)* than necessary in his monastery. The cellarer can do a lot toward defusing touchy situations by functioning in a "calm and gentle way." Still, he is not to play the doormat by caving in to improper requests and illegitimate pressures.

December 1

Let the abbot have equal charity toward all, and let him apply the same discipline to all, depending on their merits. (RB 2.22)

Benedict has packed a whole philosophy of spiritual leadership into this one verse. It is of course deeply paradoxical. On the one hand, the abbot is to maintain a completely even-handed level of love and discipline, which seems to imply the same approach to all. Yet in the next breath, he adds "depending on their merits." It is interesting to note that Benedict has quietly dropped out a passage in the Rule of the Master that compares the abbot to God, whose sun shines on both the good and the bad alike (see Matt 5:45). That kind of radical egalitarian attitude is indeed found in the Sermon on the Mount, but Benedict has seen how it worked out in the Rule of the Master. For in that Rule, it turns out that *nobody* but the abbot has any status! So the Master resembles the Russian communists, who attempted with disastrous results to create a classless society. Benedict has backed off. He realizes that merit needs to be taken into account. Peace and joy may not depend entirely on reward, but they are certainly helped thereby.

December 2

Because they fear the Lord, they are not impressed by their own good performance, for they know that what is good in them could only have come about through the Lord. (RB Prol. 29)

Periodically in his Prologue, Benedict breaks away from his commentary on the psalms to issue a warning against what we might call a "theology of works." Since the Prologue is basically a call to action, it could be misinterpreted as a claim that our salvation ultimately depends on our action. While it is true that "God will not save us without us" (Augustine), it is still God who saves us and not we ourselves. The danger with emphasizing "performance," as Benedict (following the Master) does in the Prologue, is that it could give the impression that strenuous activity is the end and goal of the monastic life. It is

not; that is union with God. We may find the comment "Because they fear the Lord" somewhat confusing and even off-
putting, but in traditional biblical language, it means that I
fully recognize that God is God—and I am not. This verse goes
even further: God alone can be seen as the source of the good;
any good "performance" on our part is strictly dependent on
God.

December 3

*It is the master's job to speak and teach; the disciple is to keep silent
and listen.* (RB 6.6)

This is a maxim that seems to come from the world of desert
monasticism (Egypt, fourth–fifth century). In this movement,
based on the pedagogical ideas of Origen of Alexandria, spiritual competence was greatly valued, and those who were
known as "masters" attracted followers to themselves. At least
theoretically, the disciple expected to obtain significant spiritual direction by simply *listening* to the master. Now all real
listening implies *silence* as its precondition, and that is why it is
discussed in this chapter. All traditional societies expect that
elders will be listened to by their juniors. But it should be
added that Benedict never again mentions this master/disciple
relation after chapter 6. He knows that a cenobitic monk, unlike a desert disciple, must listen to many brothers, not just
one. What is more, in a cenobium, no one is simply a teacher;
all are expected to listen *and* learn. What is more, a cenobitic
monk will have several successive abbots. If he finds one of
them is not spiritually helpful, he is still not free to leave.

December 4

The brothers should serve the needs of one another eating and drinking, so that no one need ask for anything. (RB 38.6)

Don't civilized people always watch out for the needs of others at table? It all depends on what you mean by "civilized." Perhaps some of Benedict's recruits were rough peasants who needed domestication. Those of Pachomius certainly were, so much so that he orders them to wear their hoods up so they cannot watch each other eating! (Rule of Pachomius, 29). But the thing most to be avoided at common meals is self-absorption and unconcern for others. Since the very act of eating is centered around the drive for personal survival, this is always a danger, and certain strong personalities, despite their high intelligence or even sensitivity (e.g., W.H. Auden), tend toward *fressen* (German: feeding) rather than *essen* (dining). Seen against its biblical background (see John 13), the community meal is a primary symbol of mutual love; it is a grotesque violation of this symbol to eat without concern for others.

December 5

All guests who happen to arrive should be received as Christ, for he himself will surely say, "I was a stranger and you took me in" [Matt 25:35]. Proper respect must be shown to "everyone, especially those of the household of the faith" [Gal 6:10] and pilgrims. (RB 53.1-2)

These verses have given the Benedictines a name for hospitality, which they have usually deserved. The use of Matthew 25 shows that this is simply basic Christian ethics: One must help the wayfarer. The chapter begins on a very magnanimous note: *All* guests must be received as Christ—and not just the honored benefactors of the monastery who have called ahead —all who *happen* to arrive. This demanding inclusivity sometimes pushes us to the limit; but it cannot be absolute. Is everyone welcome? Yes, but within limits: "Especially those of the household of the faith." The monastery is not just a hostel; it is a house of God. According to this verse, those who are inimical to religion or to the Catholic Church have no claim on us. I am not sure, however, Dorothy Day would have agreed.

December 6

They should compete in being obedient to one another. (RB 72.6)

For the second time in this wonderful little chapter, Benedict promotes a kind of holy competition. First we were exhorted to be the first to honor one another; now we are urged to outdo each other in obedience. In a certain sense, this is a witty, paradoxical statement, for obedience is essentially nonaggressive, noncompetitive. And here we are fighting for the last place! Of course, that is ridiculous, but a little humor is not out of place in these matters. In the previous chapter (71), Benedict began to discuss *mutual* obedience, but got sidetracked. Here, though, he flat-out recommends mutual obedience. While some look down on it as a watered-down form of asceticism, in fact it can be very demanding. To pay respectful attention to *everyone* in my orbit is not at all easy. We tend to narrow down the field, in effect ignoring some persons. This becomes especially difficult when there are competing, perhaps contrary, claims on our allegiance. This kind of obedience requires discernment, a gift of the Holy Spirit. Fundamentalism solves the problem by excluding all but one influence, thereby destroying mutual obedience.

December 7

The prioress should always put "mercy before strict justice" [Jas 2:13]
so she herself may receive the same treatment. She should hate vices,
but love the sisters. When she corrects someone, she should act
prudently and not overreact. (RB 64.9-12)

A curious feature of the Rule of Benedict is that it contains
not one but two chapters on the superior, one at the beginning
(RB 2) and the other at the end (RB 64). Since the second one is
a good deal gentler and more humane, it could be that after
many years of experience as an abbot, Benedict had second
thoughts about his youthful rigor. At any rate, chapter 64 is an
extremely pastoral, and even maternal, chapter. Built as it is on
the sayings of Augustine, it seems to come down almost every
time on the side of "mercy and not strict justice." Of course,
nuns are still sinners and the community will sometimes need
the bracing tonic of strong discipline. But if the prioress is primarily an icon of Christ, then she must first of all show forth
his qualities of divine forgiveness. Nor is this simply a theological issue; most people are motivated more by love than by
fear.

December 8

Children up to age fifteen should be carefully observed and disciplined
by all. But this should be done in a moderate and reasonable manner
. . . Anyone who flares up wildly at the children is to suffer the regular
discipline. (RB 70.4-6)

Someone might be excused for wondering why this verse is
presented for meditation. We certainly don't raise other peoples'

children in the monastery any more. In fact, in the wake of the recent scandals, we hardly dare go near a child! But we should not dismiss Benedict's advice too cavalierly, for he knows a lot about these matters. He sees that in a healthy community, the discipline of children is everybody's job. Every child should respect every adult, and vice versa. But this discipline is an art that not all adults can manage. The main virtue required is *calm steadiness.* And the thing children fear most is *arbitrariness.* If the parent or guardian really loves the child, then there will be no temptation to bend the child to one's own needs. Of course, adults can flare up out of weakness. A steady pattern of adult tyranny, however, will eventually result in disaster.

December 9

"Each person is endowed by God with a special gift, some this, some that" [1 Cor 7:7]. *Therefore it is with some uneasiness that we lay down rules for others in the matter of consumption.* (RB 40.1-2)

When Father Peter was procurator, one day he got a call from the kitchen that they were running short of eggs. Since the monastery had never purchased eggs before, Father Peter decided to check with Brother Felix, who kept the chickens. Felix said that the hens were indeed laying fewer eggs now, but he was not surprised because he had cut down on their feed. When Peter pressed him further, he pointed out that it was Lent and since these were Catholic and monastic chickens, then it was only right that they keep the regular observance like the rest. Peter was irate, but he held his temper since Felix was notoriously short on common sense. Sometimes, piety overwhelmed reason for him and caused him to do all sorts of strange things. He obediently restored the chickens to their normal rations, but it took a long time before they regained their capacity to lay eggs. Moral: Do not impose asceticism on others unless you are ready to take the consequences.

December 10

The prioress should frequently inspect the beds to see if private possessions are being kept there. And if someone is in fact found to have something she has not received from the prioress, she should be very severely punished. (RB 55.16-17)

This is the kind of verse that tends to shock outsiders who are hearing the Rule read for the first time. What on earth can it mean? It means what it says: The ancient nuns had no private rooms, only beds in a common dormitory. And even these beds were not their own. Authority regularly inspected them to check for illicit hoarding. How could people live this way? Remember that this was long before the "Age of Individualism." People did not need as much private space as we do. Nor did they need a lot of chattel. In the days before consumerism, people got along with very little. I myself lived quite happily for six years as a boarding school student without a private room or more storage than a foot-locker. The problem today is the opposite: monastic rooms full of all kinds of goods, about which the superior dares not say a word. Who will deliver us from this plague of possessions?

December 11

"Whoever exalts himself will be humbled, and whoever is humble will be exalted" [Luke 14:11]. (RB 7.1)

Since Benedict's huge chapter on humility is primarily a commentary on this gospel verse, it is worthwhile unpacking it. This appears to be a free-floating saying of Jesus that the gospels apply to different contexts. Note first that we have here a typical case of the "divine passive," where the missing subject is clearly God. In other words, God will humble and he will exalt, and anyone else who takes on that role may in fact be playing God. The passive verb "humbled" could also be translated "humiliated." Since this form of the verb is always negative in English, we hesitate to use it even of God. All the more so for human agents: no one has the right to humiliate another. But every life includes humiliations, and much depends on how we respond to these experiences. In an important sense, they say more about us than our own strategies toward humility. We can fool ourselves badly in regard to our own efforts at humility, but humiliation is never our own doing.

December 12

From Easter to November first, the number of psalms should be done as laid down above. But the lessons of the book are not to be read, owing to the shortness of the nights. (RB 10.1-2)

Sometimes the Divine Office must be shortened, whether because of the season of the year or because they arise late (RB 11) or in other extraordinary circumstances. When that happens, we must make a choice as to what is to be left out. Such a choice will depend on our priorities. For Benedict, the psalms must never be shortened and a community that is faithful to his Rule must take that seriously. But there are other considerations as well. For example, one of the most crucial innovations in the modern Office is the introduction of periods of silence between the psalms, readings and responses. This change has in effect slowed down the Office and given it a much more contemplative atmosphere. But some people seem to find public silence burdensome and they are tempted to fill it in with activity. They are tempted to shorten or even eliminate the silent pauses first when the group is pressed for time. Such persons must not be allowed to prevail.

December 13

The abbot should vary his approach according to the situation, mixing threats and coaxing, one time showing the sternness of a taskmaster and another time the tender affection of a father. (RB 2.24)

In this verse, Benedict advocates a leadership style that varies with the situation. Different situations demand different responses. This implies flexibility that all leaders simply do not have. It is said of General Beauregard of the Confederate Army that he failed as a battlefield strategist because he attempted to apply the tactics of Napoleon to every situation. In the verses that follow, the writer admits that some persons need to be approached subtly and reasonably, while others only respond to fairly blunt, even harsh, demands. It is a little hard to imagine these latter as members of a monastic community, but at least the point is clear: everyone cannot be dealt with in the same fashion. Note that this has nothing to do with personal likes and dislikes. The abbot may be strongly attracted to a rough and ready monk, but he will still have to find effective ways of guiding him toward his spiritual goal. Conversely, he may find it difficult to work with delicate personalities, but he still must use gentle means.

December 14

They heap praise on the Lord, who is at work in them, saying with the prophet: "Not to us, Lord, not to us, but to your name give the glory" [Ps 113:9 (115:1)]. (RB Prol. 30)

This verse repeats Benedict's frequent point in the Prologue: God is the true author of the good, even though we may be his agents. Here, though, the issue is "glory" or prestige. The psalmist wants to make sure that God receives full credit for what he has done for and through Israel. For if the credit is mistakenly ascribed by the nations to Israel, then the whole process is subverted. This in no way involves Israel's *denial* of her favored status or her considerable achievement. As long as the glory is given to God, then Israel's part in it should not be denied. When Benedict talks of "heaping praise on the Lord," he is providing us with a rare glimpse of his theology of prayer. For him, it also means the lavish praise of God for his mighty deeds among us. Compared to recent Catholic spirituality this may seem a bit impersonal, but it is perhaps the chief reason we pray the psalms at every Office.

December 15

As for crude jokes and idle chatter aimed at arousing laughter, we put an absolute clamp on them in all places. (RB 6.8)

Although there is nothing unusual about warning monks to avoid dirty jokes, we must admit that our translation "crude jokes" is already an interpretation of the term *scurrilitates*. What worries us is Benedict's apparent allergy to humor, which is generally seen by modern people as a sign of mental health. The fact is that there is much we do not understand about ancient sensibilities. For example, some commentators have suggested that what Benedict was really opposed to was ribaldry, not merriment. Since for the ancients, jokes were virtually synonymous with dirty jokes, better to eliminate them from the monastery. Although it is true that the written comedies we have from those times are filled with smutty jokes, this does not prove the point. And it should be admitted that low morale and depression are occupational hazards in ascetical societies like monasteries. When asked why he allowed conversation at all meals, an Italian abbot said he preferred to break the letter of the Rule rather than pay hospital bills.

December 16

The sisters should be issued clothing fit for the circumstances and climate where they live . . . Therefore, the prioress must be sensitive to these matters . . . The nuns should not worry over the color or texture of these things. They should simply use what is available in the region where they live, or what can be bought cheaply. (RB 55.1, 3, 7)

To someone who followed the "clothes wars" that erupted in convents after Vatican II, these verses of the Holy Rule might be surprising. Instead of the fierce passions that sometimes drove the battles over the veil and so forth, here we hear the voice of common sense: use what is fit for the climate; use what is easy to procure; don't be anxious about the color and texture of these things. It could be that Our Holy Father is insufficiently aware of the symbolic importance of clothing. Still, it is also clear that he is more committed to religious poverty than those convents that thought that cost was no concern as long as one "looked holy." And above all, it is inconceivable that Benedict would have allowed this issue to wound charity and virtually ruin some communities.

December 17

As soon as guests are announced, the superior or the sisters should hurry to meet them with every mark of love . . . The greeting itself ought to manifest complete humility toward guests on arrival or departure: by a nod of the head or a complete prostration on the ground. (RB 53.3, 7)

We may be puzzled by these rather extravagant gestures of welcome, but they are typical of ancient biblical hospitality. See especially the lovely story of Abraham, Sarah and the Three Men in Genesis 18. Another source for these verses seems to be the *History of the Monks of Egypt* (ch. 7), which describes the welcome accorded by hermits to their guests. The hospitality ethic of the Egyptian hermits was in direct continuity with that of the Eastern desert, where refusal of hospitality could spell death for the wayfarer. In addition to this, the attitude of humility and the gesture of prostration indicate that Benedict sees these matters with the eyes of faith. For him, the guest is Christ in a special form: needy, vulnerable, dependent. The precise form hospitality ought to take in our day can be debated; our obligation to see Christ in the guest cannot.

December 18

They should support each other's weaknesses of body or character with the greatest patience. (RB 72.5)

It has been said that with almost every verse in chapter 72, the adverb is the key. That certainly seems to be the case here with the word "patience." It is not merely that, but the superlative degree: "the greatest patience." Since Benedict makes it quite clear he expects that his monastery will have an abundant supply of weaknesses, some means has to be found to cope with this situation. That is where patience comes in. We should not assume that this just means stolid resignation, "putting up with each other." In fact, the word patience turns up in many significant texts of the Rule. Perhaps the most theologically important one is verse 50 of the Prologue: "We will participate in the passion of Christ through patience so as to deserve to be companions with him in his kingdom." This astonishing verse claims that true Christian patience is actually a participation in the passion and death of Christ. What higher valuation could be given to patience? Not only that: it leads straight to heaven. And from the practical point of view, patience is the only way we can live together without killing each other.

December 19

One must note whether [the novice] really seeks God, and whether he is serious about the Work of God, obedience and hardships. (RB 58.7)

When there were larger novitiates, a second monk, called "*socius*," was assigned to help the novice master with the work.

This monk, who was often a junior himself, functioned as a companion, working with the novices and sharing their everyday concerns. Frater Matthias was a typical *socius*, young, mischievous and always looking for "hard things" or menial work for the novices. They knew that half of it was busy work of no significance, but on the other hand, Matthias was sometimes hard pressed to find any work at all for them. One of their regular jobs was cleaning the bathrooms. This had to be done the right way, which required special instruction by Matthias. The senior novice went first. He was Frater Jude, a no-nonsense farm boy who had performed far worse tasks in the cow barn at home. "What about this hard stuff in the toilet?" he asked. "Oh, you scrape that off with your fingernail," said Matt. "My God, there ought to be a better way to do it than that—even in the novitiate!"

December 20

"Sinners should be publicly rebuked so others will experience fear"
[1 Tim 5:20]. (RB 70.3)

Contemporary people are often so sensitive that to rebuke them in front of others is to inflict major punishment. Of course, Benedict usually wants correction to take place first in private (RB 23; see Matt 18). But here in chapter 70 there is no private warning. Perhaps that is because the offense is so public: usurpation of the power to punish others. An added factor here may be the famous Mediterranean shame and honor culture, where life is lived mainly in public. In that world, which was Benedict's world, most human transactions assume an audience. Obviously, those witnessing a rebuke can hardly help reflecting on how it applies to themselves. Elementary psychology seems to teach that at least some people need living examples more than words to instruct them. Taking all this into account, it still seems counterproductive in our culture to make rebukes public except in the most extreme cases.

December 21

With all due regard for the weakness of the sick we think that a hemina of wine a day is enough for each person. But those to whom God gives the strength to abstain from wine should know that they will have their own special reward. (RB 40.3-4)

This kind of prescription makes little sense to a North American, at least one without an awareness that wine is almost essential in Mediterranean culture. People drink it with most meals and to go without it would be considered a great hardship. This does not mean that it is a necessity of life; nor does it mean that everyone in the south of Europe drinks wine. It would appear that the idea of strength (and weakness) is used here in two different senses. The first verse seems to imply that wine can have the effect of physically strengthening the sick. The second verse considers it a moral weakness to need wine. Concerning the details, the issue is clouded by our ignorance of just how much a *hemina* measure contained. Although the Bible never prohibits alcohol, it is well known that it tends to lessen alertness and that probably worries Benedict.

December 22

When they receive new clothes, they should always turn in the old ones. These should be kept temporarily in the wardrobe for distribution to the poor. (RB 55.9)

This single verse tells us quite a bit about the ancient nuns. First of all, Benedict makes some distinction between them and "the poor." That may rankle some people, but it was true then and it is true now: nuns are not the real poor. No one with an education and "three squares" is truly poor. Secondly, their clothing must have been quite similar to that of the common people; otherwise how could the poor wear it as seconds? This principle has been grossly violated by most Benedictines throughout the centuries. Before Vatican II, our clothing bore no resemblance to that of the ordinary person in this society. Third, Benedict does not want people hoarding clothes. But in our own time, clothing no longer wears out. Our closets fill up and we do not know what to do with the surplus. We can put it in the community clothes closet, but then it just sits there forever. Let's not waste our guilt on this matter. Take it to Goodwill!—or the like.

December 23

Let [the cellarer] watch out for his own spiritual health . . . If the community is large, let him be given help so that he can perform his duties in a calm spirit. (RB 31.8, 17)

These verses show that Benedict does not focus just on the efficiency of his officials, but is more concerned with their "spiritual health." Even though the cellarer is very much involved in material concerns, he should remember that they are never in themselves the point of his existence. Further, the community should remember this as well, so it should never simply *use* the person who proves to be able and willing to serve. The frenetic world of work in the Western world provides abundant examples of "workaholism" and its baneful effects on the human spirit. Since the monastery shares in the culture where it is located, these same values tend to creep into the cloister. Much here depends on balance: if the cellarer lets the demands and cares of his job invade the other areas of his life such as *lectio divina*, then trouble lies ahead. The abbot especially will have to beware of thrusting into this position someone who cannot maintain this balance.

December 24

The celebration of Matins and Vespers must certainly never take place without the superior reciting the whole of the Lord's Prayer as the rest all listen. This is done because of the thorns of quarrelling that often arise. (RB 13.12)

While it is not at all unusual that Benedict should want his community to pray the Lord's Prayer, it is puzzling that he arranges for the superior to recite it alone while the monks listen. He explains this format as a prophylaxis against quarrels within the community. But even that explanation leaves us in the murk. Why is it better to listen to this prayer than to recite it? Perhaps because some of them used to keep silent when the rest recited it, thinking that they somehow thereby avoided the obligation to "forgive as we forgive," the last words of the prayer. But if we must listen to those words and then respond to them, then we cannot imagine we are "off the hook." This is perhaps a fanciful explanation (by Augustine), but what remains undeniable is that Benedict wants quarrels in the community resolved as quickly as possible. "If you have a quarrel with someone, make peace before sundown." (RB 4.73)

December 25

The abbot should not neglect nor undervalue the welfare of the souls committed to him by paying more attention to fleeting, earthly, perishable things. (RB 2.33)

St. Benedict expresses this same idea several times in his two chapters on the abbot (RB 2 and 64). But the long course of Western monastic history shows that it has not been easy to observe. Perhaps the problem lies in the fact that a monastery is not just a weekend seminar on spirituality but a concrete gathering of persons with bodies as well as souls. The task of providing a roof and meals for those people is often a difficult one, and the ultimate responsibility falls on the abbot. It is not surprising that abbots of large, complex modern abbeys must give serious attention to administration. What is almost shocking is the degree of mundane financial activity that entangled even some of the earliest Cistercian abbots. This could be a consoling bit of knowledge for a modern abbot, but he must still make spiritual matters his first priority. And yet Benedict does not allow the abbot to simply delegate practical matters to the cellarer. He (the abbot) has responsibility for the whole operation.

*Paul the Apostle took no credit for his preaching, saying: "I am what
I am because of God's grace" (1 Cor 15:10), and again he says:
"Whoever boasts should boast in the Lord" [2 Cor 10:17]. (RB Prol. 32)*

One of the most obvious examples of a "spirituality of glory"
in the New Testament is Paul the Apostle. His claim that he has
a right to "boast in the Lord" may cause us to cringe a bit, since
it does not seem to tally with our idea of humility. But Paul is a
Jew, not a twenty-first century Nordic Christian, and as such
he follows quite naturally the spirituality of the Psalms. For the
Jews, there was no false sense of humility. They were good,
and they knew it! But they also understand that they are mere
agents of God, so it was to God that the glory must be directed.
In the same sense, Paul thinks he is doing the most important
thing in the world when he preaches—or rather, God is doing
this wonder through him. Admittedly, this spirituality walks a
tight line, for it easily slips over into self-adulation.

December 27

*As for the goods of the monastery, whether it be tools or clothing or
anything else, the abbot should assign brothers of reliable life and habits
and entrust to them, as he sees fit, these objects to be cared for and
collected. (RB 32.1)*

Father Rupert was not happy to come home. He was eighty-
four years old and could no longer do parish work, but he
treasured his independence. Above all, he treasured his car.
And so he simply did not turn in the keys to the cellarer, and

the car sat unused in the parking lot for everyone to contemplate. Once the cellarer asked the old man when he planned to turn in the keys, but Rupert said that he was planning a major vacation trip to the West Coast. After a year or so, he went to the abbot with his plans, but the latter begged him not to try to drive that far all alone. Rupert could not be deterred. He said that he needed the car for his golf clubs, even though he had not played in almost twenty years. Everybody held their breath when he drove out of the yard and soon the reports began to filter back: he hit a deer in Montana and side-swiped a truck in Oregon. Outside Bakersfield, the brakes gave out (he said) and the car ended up a thousand feet off the freeway with no front wheels. He came home on crutches with a bandage around his head.

December 28

We read that wine is no drink for monks. Yet since monks nowadays cannot be convinced of this, let us at least agree not to drink too much, but sparingly. "For wine makes even the wise go astray" [Sir 19:2]. (RB 39.6-7)

What Benedict has read is *The Lives of the Fathers*, 5.4, 31, a text from the Egyptian desert tradition. If he would have read a little more widely, he would have seen that the same book tells of hermits drinking wine. But he is probably not too interested in detailed history. His argument here might be termed "golden-age thinking" in which one claims perfect virtue for the earliest founders, so as to raise the sights of contemporaries. Benedict also says that the first monks recited the entire Psalter every day (18.25). Perhaps a few of them did, but it was still considered the exception, not the rule. Still, Benedict does not push too hard at the limits. He cites perfection in order to demand a reasonable norm: no drunkenness. The reader who wonders why the old monks had to drink wine at all should note that almost everybody in Mediterranean culture uses wine as a matter of course. To abstain from it is considered barbaric.

December 29

The prioress, as well as the whole community, should wash the feet of all guests. After they have washed the feet of the guests, the nuns should say this verse: "We have received, O God, your mercy in the midst of your temple" [Ps 47(48):10]. (RB 53.13-14)

Among the various rituals prescribed by Benedict toward guests, the washing of feet would seem to be the least acceptable in our day and our culture. People no longer do things like that. Nevertheless, it was standard procedure in the warm climate of the Mediterranean when people still went barefoot. At any rate, the significance of the gesture is clear: the community welcomes the guests and does what it can to make them comfortable. But there is more here. In the psalm verse that follows, the nuns make the remarkable claim that they have received God's mercy in this gesture. Shouldn't they say that the *guests* have received God's mercy? But the nuns are reminded of their own plea on the day of profession: "Receive me, O Lord, and I shall live!" (see RB 58). So the nuns are not householders grudgingly admitting guests to God's house. They affirm that they themselves remain guests in God's house.

December 30

That is, "They should outdo one another in showing respect"
[Rom 12:10]. (RB 72.4)

Although it is grammatically awkward, we include "That is" at the beginning of this verse to show that it is an appositive that explains what came before. And that is curious, since what came before is "the warmest love." Aren't respect and love almost opposed ideas? Apparently not. Notice that the nuns are urged here to "outdo one another" in showing honor. This has a way of ratcheting up the energy level. But we still have to ask how *honor* relates to *amor*. Well, if *amor* connotes the fire of love, *honor* connotes its long-term implementation. To put this into graphic terms, it is a polite and respectful thing to close doors quietly, but it is also a form of love for those who would suffer from my boorishness. Since cenobitic monastic life goes on year after year, this issue of respect becomes more and more relevant. We can show romantic warmth for a few months, but a quarter of a century of steady respect is more feasible and more appreciated. And we might add that "human rights" are basically a matter of due respect for the other.

December 31

If someone makes a mistake when chanting a psalm, response, antiphon or lesson, unless he makes humble satisfaction right then and there before all, he should suffer a more severe punishment. (RB 45.1)

It was a strange system. Before Vatican II, the Divine Office was so complicated that it took the novices weeks to learn how to maneuver through it. The Breviary had lots of ribbons, and each had to be correctly positioned to allow instant accessibility. That was because the novices, in one monastery, had to serve as prayer leaders from the day they arrived. To make matters worse, the other monks did not help them out when they stumbled; they jumped in with the correct intonation and that meant that the novice had to "kneel out" after the Office. It was a system that guaranteed tension, frustration and even nightmares for the novices. But for a certain kind of senior monk, the kind that thrives on other peoples' mistakes, it was a picnic. One day, however, Father Maurus jumped in with the wrong intonation. He was too proud to kneel out, but the abbot paid him a personal visit afterward in his room.

Index

3.2: February 10
3.3: January 1
3.4: January 14; September 18
3.5: February 2
3.6: January 27
3.12-13: February 8
4.1-9: February 20
4.10-19: March 3
4.16: April 12
4.20-28: March 15
4.25: May 5
4.28: February 1
4.29-33: March 26
4.42-43: April 7
4.44-47: April 19
4.46: February 25
4.48-50: April 30
4.51-54: May 12
4.53-54: January 19
4.55-57: May 24
4.59-61: June 5
4.61: February 13
4.64: June 12
4.68: July 13
4.72: June 28
4.73: January 6
4.76: July 9
4.76-77: July 20
4.78: August 1
5.1: August 12
5.2: August 23
5.4: September 3
5.6, 15: September 14
5.9: September 25
5.12: October 6
5.13: October 17
5.14, 16: October 28
6.1: November 9
6.2-3: November 21
6.6: December 3

6.8: December 15
7.1: December 11
7.4: October 7
7.6: May 8
7.10: June 17
7.11: January 10
7.13: January 22
7.19-20: February 5
7.21: February 17
7.23: February 29
7.29: May 30
7.30: May 18
7.31-32: March 12
7.34: March 24
7.35: April 4; April 16
7.39: April 28
7.44: May 9
7.46: May 21
7.49: June 2
7.51: June 18
7.54: June 29
7.55: July 17
7.56: July 28
7.59: August 9
7.60: August 20
7.62: August 31
7.63: September 11
7.64: September 22
7.67: October 3
7.68: October 14
7.69: October 18
7.70: November 6
8.3: November 18
9.8: November 22
10.1-2: December 12
13.12: December 24
15.3: November 3
16.5: July 21
18.22-23: February 4
18.25: January 2

19.6-7: January 15
20.1: October 22
20.1-2: January 28
20.2: February 9
20.3: February 21
20.5: September 26
21.3-4: March 16
21.5-6: March 27
22.4, 7: May 1
22.5-6: April 8
22.6, 8: April 20
22.8: October 10
23.1: May 13
23.3-5: May 25
24.1: June 6
25.1-2, 4: June 25
27.1: July 6
27.2-3: July 16
27.3: July 27
27.5: July 14
27.5-6: August 8
27.6-7: August 19
27.8-9: August 30
28.1: September 10
28.2-3: September 21
28.7-8: October 2
29.1: October 13
30.2: October 25
31.1: November 5
31.2: November 17
31.6-7: November 30
31.8, 17: December 23
31.10: November 23
31.12: July 10
31.13: April 24
31.13-14: March 8
31.15: January 3
31.16: January 16
31.17: December 23
31.19: January 29

32.1: December 27
32.1-2: January 9
32.3: January 21
32.4-5: March 5
33.1-2: March 17
33.3: February 28
33.4: March 11
33.5: April 21
33.6: May 2
34.0: April 15
34.1-2: May 26
34.3-4: June 7
34.5: May 20
34.6: June 30
35.1-2: June 13; June 24
35.3-4: July 5
35.12-13: August 13
35.15: August 24
36.1-3: February 22
36.4: March 31
36.4-5: September 15
36.7: March 4; September 20
36.8: September 9
37.1: October 1
38.1: November 10
38.5: October 24
38.6: December 4
39.1-2: November 15
39.3: November 28
39.6-7: December 28
40.1-2: August 29; December 9
40.3-4: December 21
40.6-7: September 4;
    November 26
40.8-9: July 15
41.4-5: March 28
41.8: September 7
42.1, 8, 10: January 4
42.3-4: January 17
43.1, 3: January 30

43.3-4: February 11
43.4: June 22
43.5: July 3
43.7: February 23
43.8-9: March 6
43.13, 15: March 18
43.19: March 29
44.1: April 10
44.5-6: April 22
45.1: December 31
45.1-2: May 3
46.1-4: May 15
46.5-6: May 27
47.1: June 8
47.3-4: June 20
48.1: July 1
48.3-4: July 11
48.7-8: August 3
48.15-16: August 14
48.17-18, 21: July 22
48.22-23: August 25
49.1-2: September 5
49.6: September 16
49.7: September 27
49.8: August 7
49.8-9: October 8
50.1, 3-4: October 20
51.1-2: October 30
52.1, 5: November 11
52.4: November 24
53.1-2: December 5
53.3, 7: December 17
53.13-14: December 29
53.15: October 19
53.21: May 14
53.24: February 16
54.1, 3: August 2
55.1, 3, 7: December 16
55.9: December 22
55.13-14: May 16

55.16-17: December 10
55.18: April 23
55.18-19: May 4
55.20-21: November 29
57.1: September 29
57.1-3: November 16
57.4, 7-8: November 4
57.4-6: April 11
58.1: January 8; July 24
58.3-4: March 30
58.5-6: January 20
58.7: December 19
58.7-8: February 3
58.13-14: March 19
58.17-18: February 15
58.19-20: March 7
58.21: February 24
58.22-23: February 12
58.24-25: January 31
58.26: January 18
58.27-28: February 27
59.1-2: August 5
60.1-2: March 22
61.1: April 26
61.2, 4: April 2
61.8-10: March 9
61.10: March 21
61.13-14: April 14
62.8-10: May 7
63.1-2: May 19
63.4: April 1
63.8: November 1
63.10-11, 15: May 31
63.11: April 13; November 13
63.13: June 9
63.16-17: April 25
64.1: June 10
64.3-5: June 23
64.9: July 4
64.9-12: January

64.12-14: January 5; January 14
64.15: January 7
64.16: January 26; February 14
64.18: May 6
64.19: July 25
64.21-22: February 26
65.1-2: August 6
65.14-15: August 17
65.15: May 17
65.16: May 29
66.1, 3: August 28
66.4-5: September 8
66.6-7: September 19
67.5: September 30
68.1-2: October 11
68.2-3: October 23
68.4-5: November 2
69.1-2: November 14
70.1-2: November 27
70.3: December 20
70.4-6: December 8
71.1-2: March 23
71.1, 3-4: July 26

71.3-4: August 27
71.6-8: April 9
71.7: August 16
72.1-2: April 3
72.3: August 18
72.4: December 30
72.5: December 18
72.6: December 6
72.7: March 20; November 25
72.8: November 12
72.9: October 31
72.10: October 21
72.11: October 9
72.12: September 28
73.0: September 6
73.1: September 17
73.2: August 15; August 26
73.3: August 4
73.4: July 23
73.5: July 2; July 12
73.6-7: June 21
73.8: June 11
73.9: May 28